Key Stage 2 Maths

WORKBOOK 6

Numerical Reasoning Technique

Dr Stephen C Curran

with Katrina MacKay

Edited by Andrea Richardson

ae
TUITION

Accelerated Education Publications Ltd

Contents

12. Percentages   Pages

1. What is a Percentage?   3-5
2. Percentages & Fractions   6-10
3. Percentages & Decimals   10-11
4. Fractions, Decimals & Percentages   12-15
5. Percentage Calculations   15-21
6. % Calculations Summary   22
7. Problem Solving   23-24

13. Ratio

1. What is a Ratio?   25-26
2. Proportion   26-27
3. Amount to Ratio   27-28
4. Ratio to Amount   28-31
5. Ratios & Fractions   31-33
6. Ratios & Percentages   33-36
7. Maps & Scale Drawings   36-40
8. Problem Solving   41-42

14. Probability

1. What is Probability?   43-44
2. Equal Probabilities   44-46
3. Possible Outcomes   46-47
4. Calculating Probability   48-50
5. The Probability Scale   50-52
6. Expressing Probability   52-54
7. Problem Solving   54-55

15. Lines & Angles

1. Types of Line   56-58
2. Types of Angle   58-62
3. Line & Angle Relationships   63-70
4. Measuring Angles   70-72
5. Bearings & Directions   73-74

Chapter Twelve
PERCENTAGES
1. What is a Percentage?

A **Percentage** is a number out of **100**.

A percentage is shown by this symbol: **%**

One hundred per cent (100%) is the whole amount.

Percentages that are less than **100%** represent part of an amount. For example, **50%** is **half** of the total.

Percentages are often seen in shops and banks and advertisements.

Percentages can be shown on a grid of **100** squares.

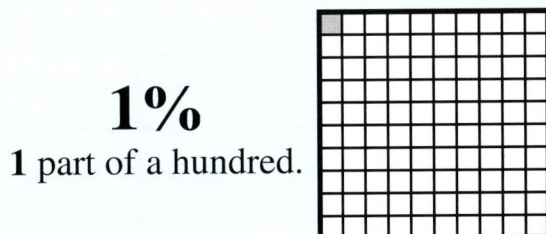

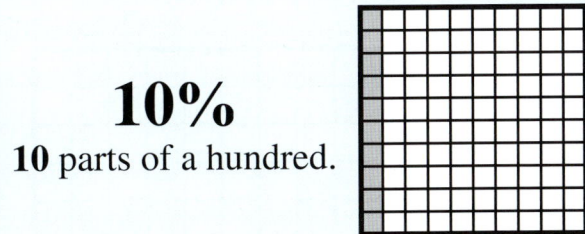

1%
1 part of a hundred.

10%
10 parts of a hundred.

Example: What percentage of this grid is shaded?

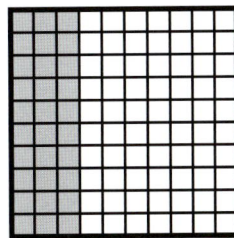

Count the number of shaded squares. There are **30** shaded squares out of a total of **100** squares. This means **30%** of the grid is shaded.

Answer: **30%**

Exercise 12: 1

Count the squares and write the % shaded:

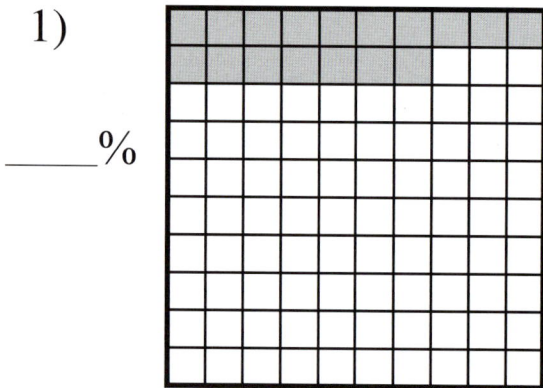

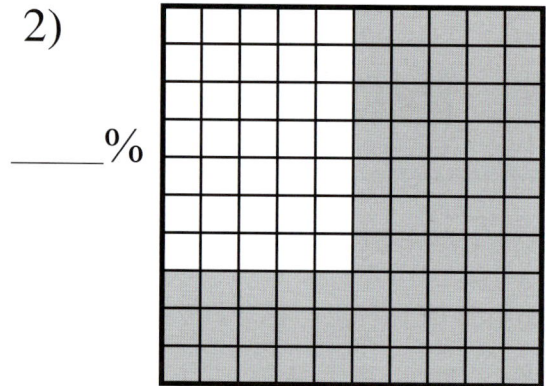

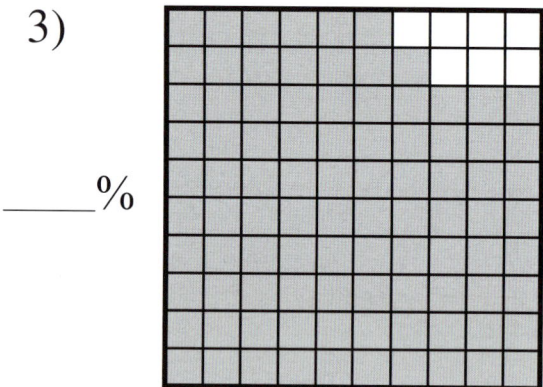

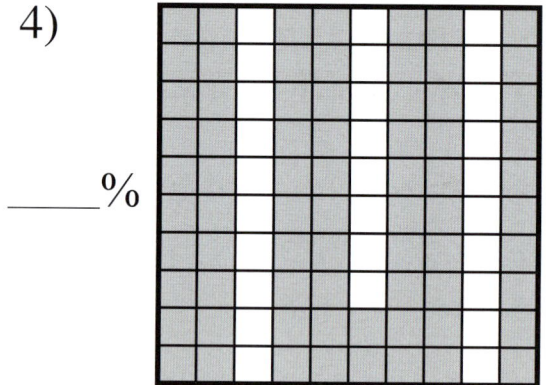

1)
_____%

2)
_____%

3)
_____%

4)
_____%

Shade in the percentage:

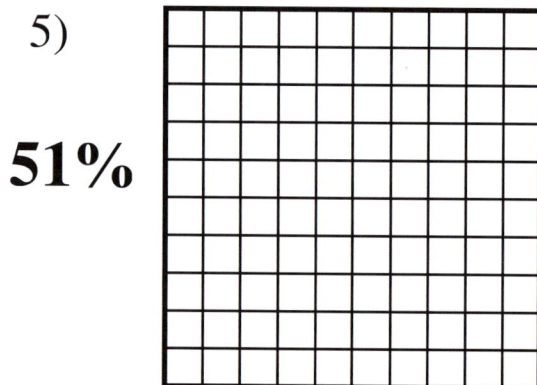

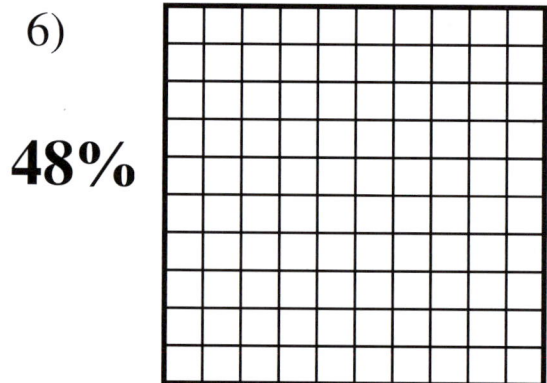

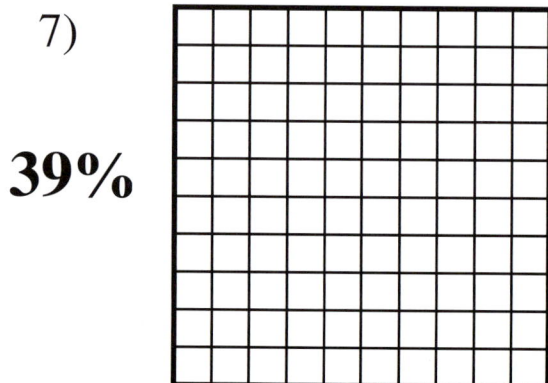

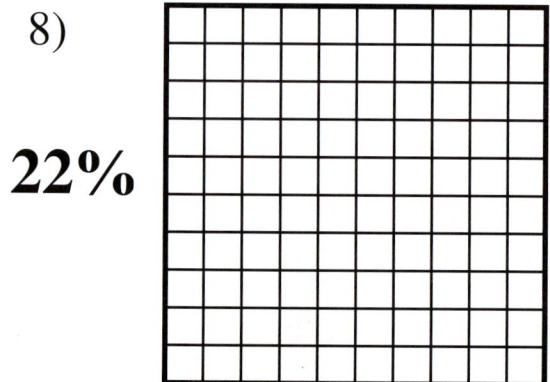

5)

51%

6)

48%

7)

39%

8)

22%

9) An addition sign has been
   shaded on a grid of **100**
   squares.

   What percentage of the grid
   does it take up? _____%

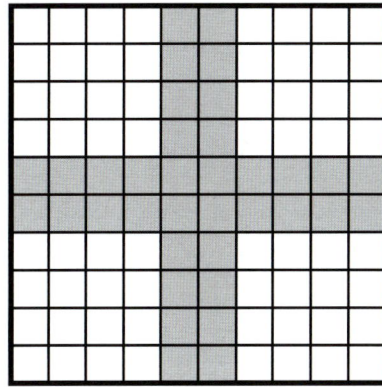

10) Shade in a multiplication sign on the grid below:

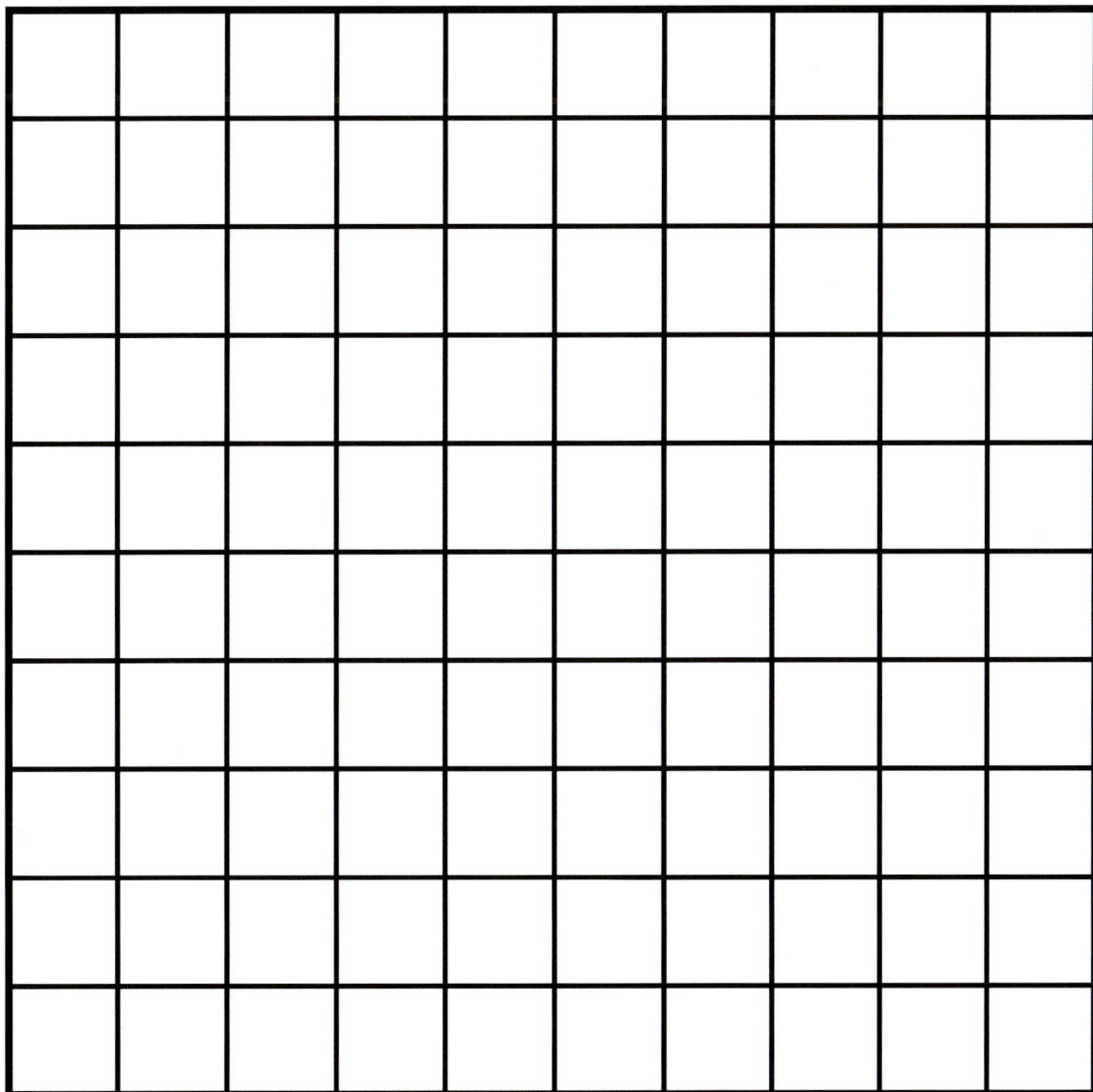

What percentage of the grid does it take up?

_____%

2. Percentages & Fractions

Percentages can be written as **Fractions**, because they represent parts of a total or whole one. For example:

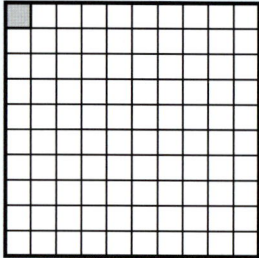

$$1\% = \frac{1}{100}$$

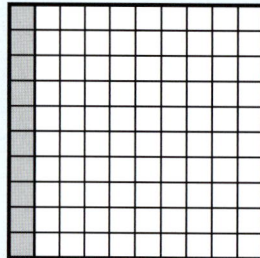

$$10\% = \frac{10}{100} = \frac{1}{10}$$

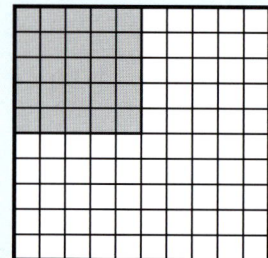

$$25\% = \frac{25}{100} = \frac{1}{4}$$

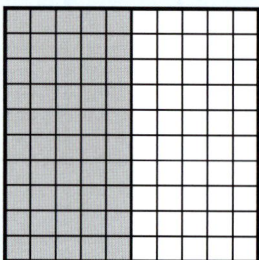

$$50\% = \frac{50}{100} = \frac{1}{2}$$

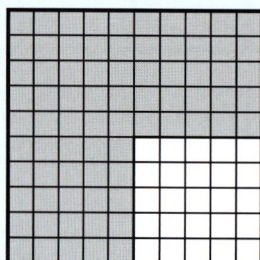

$$75\% = \frac{75}{100} = \frac{3}{4}$$

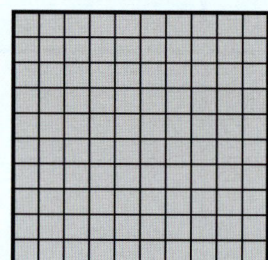

$$100\% = \frac{100}{100} = 1 \text{ whole}$$

Example: Write the percentage of the first grid and its equal fraction for the second grid.

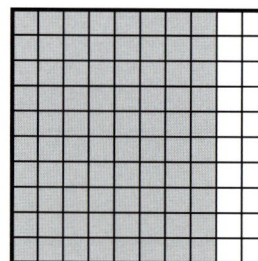 $=$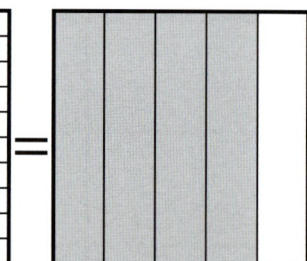

% $\frac{?}{?}$

Step 1 - Count the number of shaded squares. There are **80** shaded squares out of a total of **100** squares. This means **80%** of the first grid is shaded.

Step 2 - There are **4** shaded parts in the second grid, out of a total of **5** parts.
This means the equivalent fraction is $\frac{4}{5}$.

Answer: $80\% = \frac{80}{100} = \frac{4}{5}$

Exercise 12: 2

Write the missing equivalent percentage or fraction:

Score

1)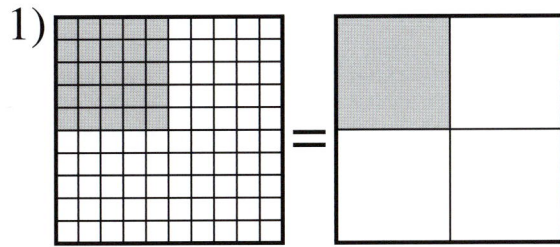

25% = ——

2)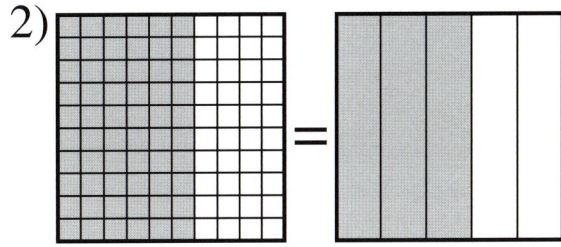

—— = $\frac{3}{5}$

3)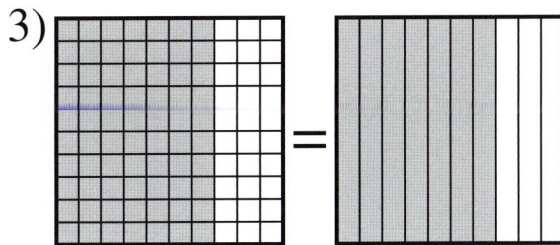

—— = $\frac{7}{10}$

4)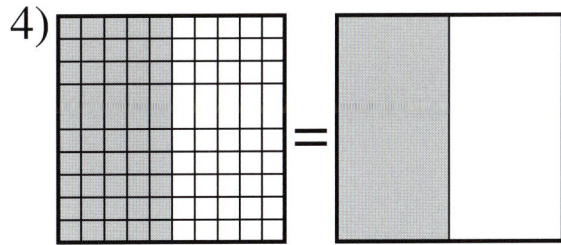

50% = ——

5)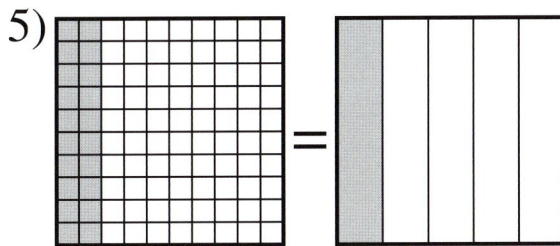

20% = ——

6)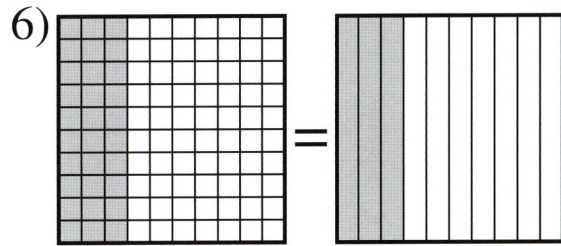

—— = $\frac{3}{10}$

7)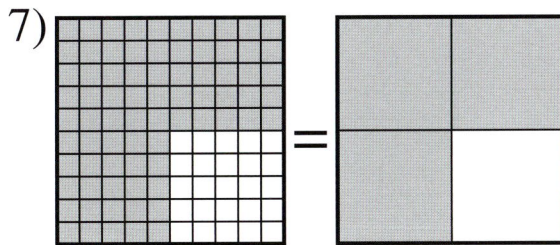

75% = ——

8)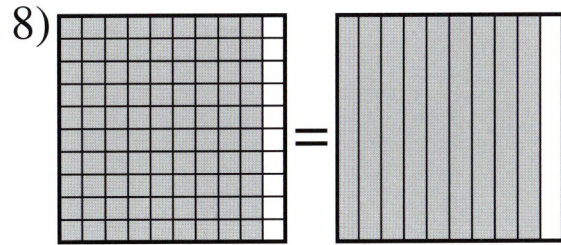

—— = $\frac{9}{10}$

9)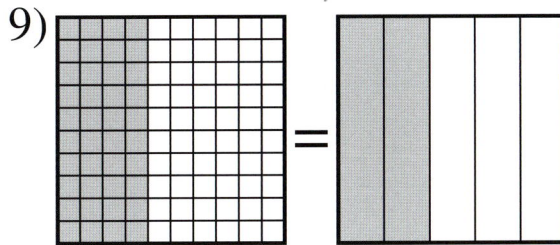

40% = ——

10)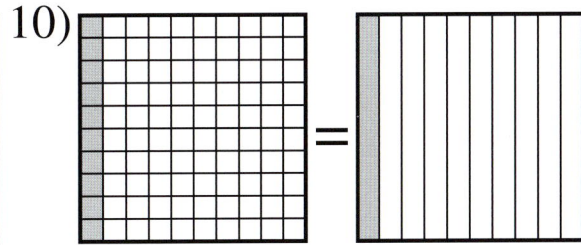

—— = $\frac{1}{10}$

As it is not always possible to draw grids and diagrams, it is better to use a method for converting percentages to fractions and fractions to percentages.

a. Changing Percentages to Fractions

Example: | Convert **40%** to a fraction. |

Step 1 - Write **40%** as a fraction over **100**.
This is $\frac{40}{100}$.

Step 2 - Simplify $\frac{40}{100}$ by dividing by **20**.

$$\frac{\cancel{40}^{\,2}}{\cancel{100}^{\,5}} = \frac{2}{5}$$

This is represented on the grid.

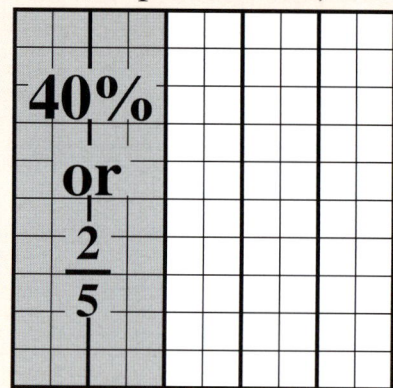

40 hundredths
(**40** parts of **100**)

40%
or
$\frac{2}{5}$

Answer: $\frac{2}{5}$

Exercise 12: 3 Change from % to fraction:

1)
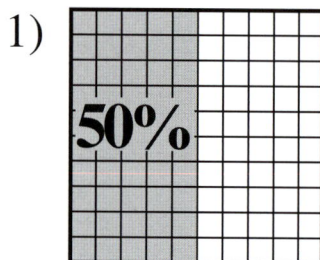

Simplify

$\frac{50}{100}$

= _____

2)
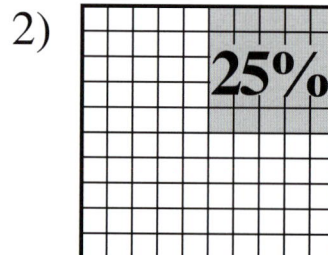

Simplify

$\frac{25}{100}$

= _____

3)
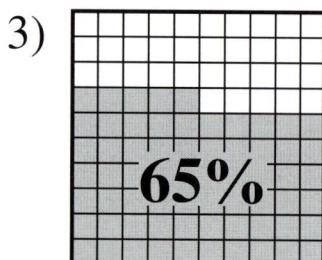

Simplify

= _____

4)
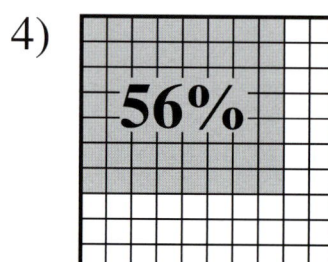

Simplify

= _____

5) 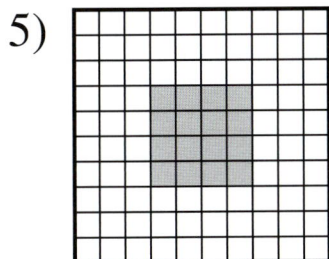 = _____

6) 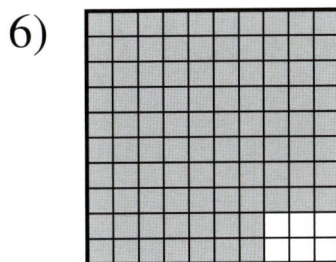 = _____

7) **38%** = _____

8) **76%** = _____

9) **45%** = _____

10) **80%** = _____

b. Changing Fractions to Percentages

Example: | Change $\frac{2}{5}$ into a percentage.

This requires the same method as multiplying fractions. To change a fraction to a percentage, the fraction must be multiplied by **100**.

Step 1 - Set out the calculation: $\frac{2}{5} \times \frac{100}{1}$

Remember, a whole number can be changed to a fraction by writing it over **1**, so **100** becomes $\frac{100}{1}$.

Step 2 - Cancel the fractions.

$$\frac{2}{{}^1 5} \times \frac{100^{20}}{1} \quad \text{which is} \quad \frac{2}{1} \times \frac{20}{1}$$

Step 3 - Multiply the fractions.

$$\frac{2}{1} \times \frac{20}{1} \qquad \begin{array}{l} 2 \times 20 = \mathbf{40} \\ \overline{} \\ 1 \times 1 \;\; = \;\; 1 \end{array}$$

40 hundredths
(40 parts of **100**)

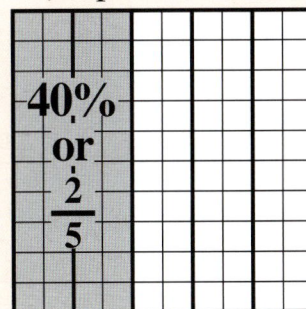

$\frac{40}{1}$ is the same as **40** or **40%**.

This is represented on the grid.

Answer: **40%**

Exercise 12: 4 Change from fraction to %:

1)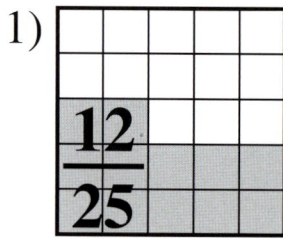

Cancel

$$\frac{12}{25} \times \frac{100}{1}$$

= _____%

2)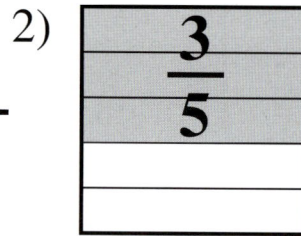

Cancel

$$\frac{3}{5} \times \frac{100}{1}$$

= _____%

3)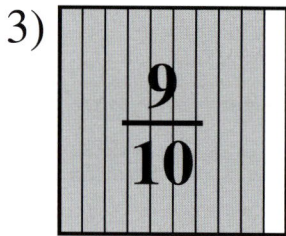

Cancel

= _____%

4)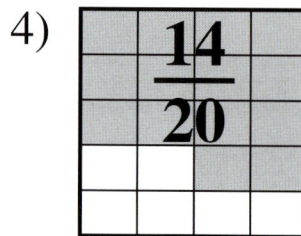

Cancel

= _____%

5)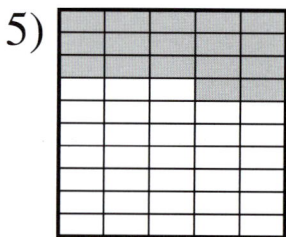

= _____%

6)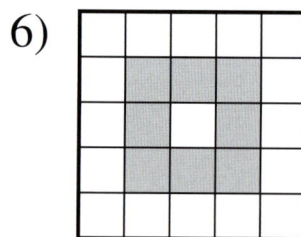

= _____%

7) $\frac{11}{20}$ = _____%

8) $\frac{27}{50}$ = _____%

9) $\frac{4}{25}$ = _____%

10) $\frac{41}{50}$ = _____%

3. Percentages & Decimals

Percentages can be converted to **Decimals** as they are parts of **100**. For example, **63%** is **63** hundredths (**63** parts of **100**) as shown on the grid. **0.63** is **63** hundredths. Therefore, **63%** is the same as **0.63**.

As percentages are parts of **100**, changing percentages to decimals and decimals to percentages is very simple.

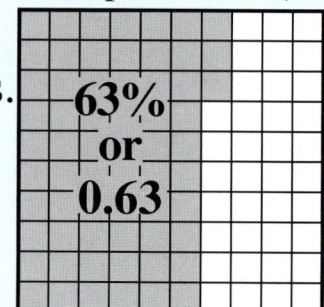

63 hundredths
(63 parts of 100)

63% or 0.63

a. Changing Percentages to Decimals

Example: | Convert **49%** to a decimal.

Divide the percentage by **100**.
Move the decimal point
two places to the left.

2 places left

⟵

49.0% ⟶ **0.49**

Answer: **0.49**

Exercise 12: 5   Convert % to decimal:

Score

1) **27%** = _____
2) **45%** = _____
3) **7%** = _____
4) **79%** = _____
5) **39%** = _____
6) **42%** = _____
7) **16%** = _____
8) **68%** = _____
9) **12%** = _____
10) **30%** = _____

b. Changing Decimals to Percentages

Example: | Convert **0.28** to a percentage.

Multiply the decimal by **100**.
Move the decimal point
two places to the right.

2 places right

⟶

0.28 ⟶ **28.0%**

Answer: **28%**

Exercise 12: 6   Convert decimal to %:

Score

1) **0.01** = _____%
2) **0.25** = _____%
3) **0.56** = _____%
4) **0.8** = _____%
5) **0.93** = _____%
6) **0.14** = _____%
7) **0.37** = _____%
8) **0.62** = _____%
9) **0.48** = _____%
10) **0.79** = _____%

4. Fractions, Decimals & Percentages

a. Useful Equivalents

Fractions, Decimals & Percentages are all ways of representing amounts. The same amount can be shown in three different ways.

The table shows useful equivalent conversions of fractions, decimals and percentages. It can be used to work out simple conversions. For example:

$$\frac{3}{10} = 0.3 = 30\%$$

Fraction	Decimal	Percentage
$\frac{1}{100}$	0.01	1%
$\frac{1}{20}$	0.05	5%
$\frac{1}{10}$	0.1	10%
$\frac{1}{5}$	0.2	20%
$\frac{1}{4}$	0.25	25%
$\frac{1}{2}$	0.5	50%
$\frac{3}{4}$	0.75	75%

Example: Write the equivalent decimal and percentage for this fraction.

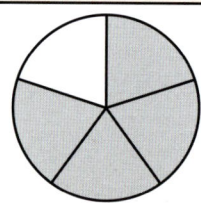

The shaded parts of the circle are $\frac{4}{5}$ of the whole.

Step 1 - The equivalence table above shows that $\frac{1}{5}$ is equal to **0.2**.
To turn $\frac{1}{5}$ into $\frac{4}{5}$, multiply by **4**. So **0.2** must be multiplied by **4** to give **0.8**.

Step 2 - To find the percentage, multiply **0.8** by **100** (move the decimal point two places to the right) giving **80%**.

Answer: $\frac{4}{5} = 0.8 = 80\%$

Exercise 12: 7

Write the equivalent decimal and percentage:

1)

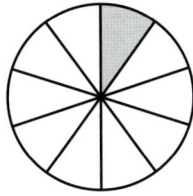

$$\frac{1}{10} = \underline{0.1} = \underline{}$$

2)

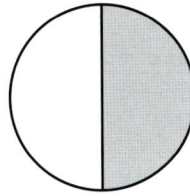

$$\frac{1}{2} = \underline{} = \underline{50\%}$$

3)

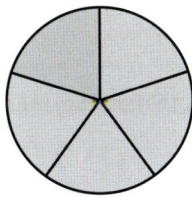

$$\underline{} = \underline{} = \underline{}$$

4)

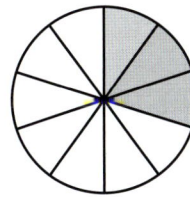

$$\underline{} = \underline{} = \underline{}$$

5)

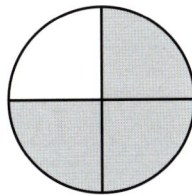

$$\underline{} = \underline{} = \underline{}$$

6)

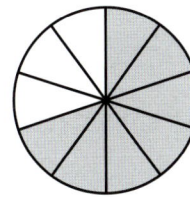

$$\underline{} = \underline{} = \underline{}$$

7)

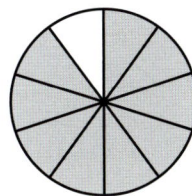

$$\underline{} = \underline{} = \underline{}$$

8)

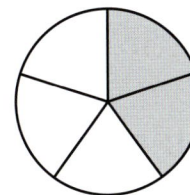

$$\underline{} = \underline{} = \underline{}$$

9)

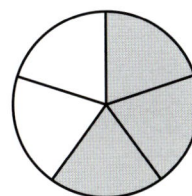

$$\underline{} = \underline{} = \underline{}$$

10)

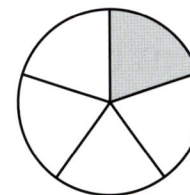

$$\underline{} = \underline{} = \underline{}$$

b. Percentages, Decimals & Fractions

When comparing the size of **Percentages**, **Decimals & Fractions**, all the amounts can be converted to percentages, decimals or fractions depending on what is most convenient.

Example	$\frac{5}{100}$	6%	0.04
Fractions	$\frac{5}{100}$	$\frac{6}{100}$	$\frac{4}{100}$
Percentages	5%	6%	4%
Decimals	0.05	0.06	0.04

Example: Put the following in size order, smallest first.

$$\frac{7}{25} \qquad 27\% \qquad 0.29$$

In this example it is easier to change everything to percentages to compare the sizes.

Step 1 - To change $\frac{7}{25}$ to a percentage, the fraction must be multiplied by **100**. $\frac{7}{25}$ is **28%**.

$$\frac{7}{25} \times \frac{100^4}{1} = \frac{28}{1}$$

A simple way to do this is to multiply the whole fraction by **4** to give it a denominator of **100**.

$$\frac{7 \times 4}{25 \times 4} = \frac{28}{100} = 28\%$$

Step 2 - Multiply **0.29** by **100** to change it to a percentage (move the decimal point two places to the right).

0.29 × 100 = 29%

Step 3 - Put the percentages in size order and then change them back to their original form.

$$27\% \qquad 28\% \qquad 29\%$$
$$\downarrow \qquad\quad \downarrow \qquad\quad \downarrow$$
$$27\% \qquad \frac{7}{25} \qquad 0.29$$

Answer: 27% $\frac{7}{25}$ 0.29

Exercise 12: 8 Answer the following:

1) Put in size order, smallest first. $\quad$ **13%** $\quad \frac{1}{10} \quad$ **0.11** = _____ _____ _____

2) Put in size order, largest first. $\quad \frac{4}{5} \quad$ **0.77** $\quad$ **81%** = _____ _____ _____

Which is smallest?

3) $\frac{17}{100}$ $\quad$ **16%** $\quad$ **0.15** _____

4) $\frac{3}{10}$ $\quad$ **0.31** $\quad$ **35%** _____

5) **0.56** $\quad$ **61%** $\quad \frac{3}{5}$ _____

6) **42%** $\quad$ **0.43** $\quad \frac{9}{20}$ _____

Which is largest?

7) $\frac{1}{4}$ $\quad$ **0.26** $\quad$ **24%** _____

8) $\frac{1}{5}$ $\quad$ **25%** $\quad$ **0.29** _____

9) $\frac{3}{5}$ $\quad$ **0.67** $\quad$ **71%** _____

10) $\frac{1}{100}$ $\quad$ **0.03** $\quad$ **5%** _____

5. Percentage Calculations

The conversion of percentages to fractions and fractions to percentages is the basis of all **Percentage Calculations**.

% to Fraction

For example, to find **60%** as a fraction:

Write it over **100**, then simplify. $\quad \dfrac{\cancel{60}^{3}}{\cancel{100}^{5}} = \dfrac{3}{5}$

Fraction to %

For example, to find $\frac{3}{5}$ as a percentage.

Multiply by **100**, then cancel. $\quad \dfrac{3}{\cancel{5}^{1}} \times \dfrac{\cancel{100}^{20}}{1} = 60\%$

a. Percentage to Amount
(i) Simple % Calculations

Finding a percentage of a given amount can be easily done for certain percentages. Use the following to find:

1%	- find one-hundredth	- **divide by 100**
10%	- find one-tenth	- **divide by 10**
20%	- find one-fifth	- **divide by 5**
25%	- find one quarter	- **divide by 4**
50%	- find one half	- **divide by 2**

Example: Find **20% of 240.**

To find **20%** is the same as finding **one-fifth**.

Divide by **5**   **240 ÷ 5 = 48**

Answer: **48**

Exercise 12: 9   Find the amount:

Score

1) **25% of 120.** _____
2) **20% of 200.** _____
3) **50% of 6p.** _____
4) **10% of £13.** _____
5) **25% of 22.** _____
6) **1% of 300.** _____
7) **10% of 450kg.** _____
8) **25% of 110.** _____
9) **1% of 500g.** _____
10) **50% of 800.** _____

(ii) Simple Two-step % Calculations

By dividing down or multiplying up, it is possible to do easy two-step calculations. For example to calculate:

4% - find **1%** then multiply by **4**.
5% - find **10%** then divide by **2**.
30% - find **10%** then multiply by **3**.
75% - find **25%** then multiply by **3**.

Example: Find **60%** of **£140**.

Step 1 - Find **10%** - divide by **10**

£140 ÷ 10 = £14

Step 2 - Find **60%** - multiply by **6**

£14 × 6 = £84

Answer: **£84**

Exercise 12: 10 Find the amount:

Score

1) **70%** of **320**. _____

2) **60%** of **300**. _____

3) **5%** of **20p**. _____

4) **30%** of **£78**. _____

5) **75%** of **62**. _____

6) **90%** of **450**. _____

7) **40%** of **900kg**. _____

8) **80%** of **700**. _____

9) **2%** of **300g**. _____

10) **9%** of **750**. _____

(iii) Basic % to Amount Calculations

There is a standard technique for finding more complex percentages. This is an easy way to find any percentage and it uses the multiplication of fractions.

For example, **1%** of **100** is **1** (this is the same as $\frac{1}{100}$ of **100**).

$$\frac{1}{{}^1\cancel{100}} \times \frac{\cancel{100}^1}{1} = 1$$

Example: $\boxed{\text{Find } \mathbf{24\%} \text{ of } \mathbf{175.}}$

To find the percentage, this calculation needs to be written as the multiplication of fractions.

Step 1 - Write the % and amount as fractions.

$$\overset{\%}{24\%} = \frac{24}{100} \qquad \overset{\text{Amount}}{175} = \frac{175}{1}$$

Step 2 - Multiply the percentage by the amount and cancel the fractions.

$$\% \longrightarrow \text{Amount}$$

$$\overset{\text{Divide by 25}}{\frac{24}{\cancel{100}\,4} \times \frac{\cancel{175}\,^{7}}{1}}$$

Step 3 - Simplify the fractions.

$$\overset{\text{Divide by 4}}{\frac{\cancel{24}\,^{6}}{\cancel{4}\,^{1}} \times \frac{7}{1}}$$

Step 4 - Multiply out the fractions.

$$\frac{6}{1} \times \frac{7}{1}$$

Answer: 42

Exercise 12: 11 Find the amount:

1) **15% of £240.** _____

$$\frac{15}{100} \times \frac{240}{1}$$

2) **85% of 40.** _____

$$\frac{85}{100} \times \frac{40}{1}$$

3) **62% of 300.** _____

4) **12% of 800cm.** _____

5) **18% of 400.** _____

6) **34% of 50.** _____

7) **70% of 70p.** _____

8) **28% of 225km.** _____

9) **90% of 90m.** _____

10) **46% of 600.** _____

b. Percentage Increase & Decrease

Amounts can be **Increased** or **Decreased** by a percentage. For example, a child's pocket money might be increased by a specific percentage.

When a shop has a sale, it might decrease the price of an item by a specific percentage such as **10%** or **25%**.

(i) Increasing Amounts by Percentage

Example: | Increase **£40** by **15%**.

Step 1 - Find **15%** of **£40**.

$$\% \longrightarrow \text{Amount}$$

$$\frac{\overset{3}{\cancel{15}}}{\underset{2}{\cancel{100}}^{\cancel{10}}} \times \frac{\overset{4}{\cancel{40}}}{1}$$

Step 2 - Add the new amount onto the original amount.

$$15\% \text{ of } £40 = £6$$

$$£40 + £6 = £46$$

Answer: **£46**

Exercise 12: 12   Increase the following:

1) **470** by **10%**.

$$\frac{10}{100} \times \frac{470}{1}$$

470 + _____ = _____

2) **600p** by **1%**.

$$\frac{1}{100} \times \frac{600}{1}$$

600p + _____ = _____

3) **820** by **50%**. _____

4) **375** by **20%**. _____

5) **180** by **5%**. _____

6) **£410** by **75%**. _____

7) **55cm** by **30%**. _____

8) **800** by **40%**. _____

9) **£210** by **25%**. _____

10) **67m** by **90%**. _____

Score

© 2016 Stephen Curran

19

(ii) Decreasing Amounts by Percentage

Example: Decrease **40** by **35%**.

Step 1 - Find **35%** of 40.

$$\% \longrightarrow \text{Amount}$$

$$\frac{\cancel{35}^{\,7}}{\cancel{100}_{\,1}^{\,5}} \times \frac{\cancel{40}^{\,2}}{1}$$

Step 2 - Subtract the new amount from the original amount.

$$35\% \text{ of } 40 = 14$$

$$40 - 14 = 26$$

Answer: **26**

Score

Exercise 12: 13   Decrease the following:

1) **625** by **20%**. _____

$$\frac{20}{100} \times \frac{625}{1}$$

625 − ____ = _____

2) **60** by **15%**. _____

$$\frac{15}{100} \times \frac{60}{1}$$

60 − ____ = _____

3) **£457** by **10%**. _____

4) **700** by **30%**. _____

5) **320cm** by **50%**. _____

6) **£170** by **2%**. _____

7) **410** by **70%**. _____

8) **720** by **25%**. _____

9) **480** by **40%**. _____

10) **659m** by **1%**. _____

c. Amount to Percentage

This involves working out what an amount represents as a percentage. The same method is used as for finding what a fraction would be if written as a percentage.

For example, **3** out of **4** as a fraction is $\frac{3}{4}$ which is **75%**. More difficult calculations are best solved using the method.

Example: | What percentage of **120** is **24**?

Step 1 - Set out the amount and % as fractions in order to multiply.

$$\text{Amount} \longrightarrow \%$$

$$\frac{24}{120} \times \frac{100}{1}$$

Step 2 - Cancel the fractions.

Divide by **10**

$$\frac{24}{\cancel{120}^{12}} \times \frac{\cancel{100}^{10}}{1}$$

Step 3 - Simplify the fractions.

Divide by **12**

$$\frac{\cancel{24}^{2}}{\cancel{12}^{1}} \times \frac{10}{1}$$

Step 4 - Multiply out the fractions.

$$\frac{2}{1} \times \frac{10}{1}$$

Answer: **20%**

Exercise 12: 14   Find the %:

1) **300** as a % of **600**. _____

$$\frac{300}{600} \times \frac{100}{1}$$

2) **50** as a % of **200**. _____

$$\frac{50}{200} \times \frac{100}{1}$$

3) **75p** as a % of **£3**. _____

4) **420g** as a % of **1kg**. _____

5) **30** as a % of **500**. _____

6) **55** as a % of **275**. _____

7) **70** as a % of **700**. _____

8) **40** as a % of **250**. _____

9) **1** as a % of **100**. _____

10) **£20** as a % of **£80**. _____

Score

6. % Calculations Summary

Percentage to Fraction becomes **Percentage to Amount**.
Fraction to Percentage becomes **Amount to Percentage**.
All percentage calculations are of two types:

either

Percentage to Amount (% → Amount)

A percentage is given and an amount has to be found.
There are three types of question:

1. Basic % to amount - e.g. Find **40%** of **£120**.
2. Increasing amount by % - e.g. Increase **£70** by **10%**.
3. Decreasing amount by % - e.g. Decrease **£80** by **25%**.

or

Amount to Percentage (Amount → %)

An amount is given and a percentage has to be found.

Basic amount to % - e.g. What % is **10** out of **160**?

Score

Exercise 12: 15 Calculate the following:

Percentage to amount questions.

1) **10%** of **280**. _____ 2) **25%** of **£136**. _____

3) **5%** of **500**. _____ 4) **20%** of **124km**. _____

5) **50%** of **390**. _____

Amount to percentage questions.

6) **48** as a % of **600**. _____ 7) **65p** as a % of **£5**. _____

8) **48** as a % of **240**. _____ 9) **135cm** as a % of **3m**. _____

10) **27** as a % of **300**. _____

7. Problem Solving

Example: In Peter's class there are **28** children. **75%** of the children have a pet. How many children in the class do not have a pet?

This is a % to amount question.

Step 1 - To find **75%**, or $\frac{3}{4}$, of **28**, first divide **28** by **4**, then multiply by **3**.

$28 \div 4 = 7$ This is **25%** of the children.

Now multiply by **3** to find **75%** of the children.
$$7 \times 3 = 21$$

This can also be solved by multiplying the fractions:

$$\frac{\overset{3}{\cancel{75}}}{\underset{1}{\cancel{100}}} \times \frac{\overset{1}{\cancel{28}}}{1}$$

Step 2 - Subtract **75%** of the children (**21**) from the total number of children (**28**) to find how many children do not have a pet.
$$28 - 21 = 7$$

Answer: **7**

Exercise 12: 16 Answer the following:

Score

1) In a class of **24** children, **25%** bring a bottle of water. How many children bring water to class? _____

2) Alice wants to bake a cake and has **250g** of butter in the fridge. The recipe requires **100g** of butter. What percentage of her butter will be used in the cake? _____

3) A gaming device usually costs **£125**. There is a **20%** sale in a local technology shop. How much will the device cost in the sale? _____

4) A medium meal in a takeaway restaurant costs **£4**. A large meal costs **10%** more. How much does a large meal cost? _____

5) There are **28** children in Mr Stone's class. **75%** own a cat. How many children do not own a cat? _____

6) Rory needs to get **65%** to pass an exam. If there are **180** questions, how many questions does he need to answer correctly to pass? _____

7) On a menu of **60** items, **15** items contain dairy products. What percentage of the menu does not contain dairy products? _____

8) Hannah wants to save **£500** to go on holiday. She has saved **£350**. What percentage of the total amount does she still need to save? _____

9) In Mrs Blount's class there are **30** children. If **20%** of them cannot swim, how many can swim? _____

10) Muskan scores **126** out of **180** marks in a test. What percentage did she get? _____

Chapter Thirteen
RATIO

1. What is a Ratio?

A **Ratio** is a way of comparing two or more amounts with each other. The amounts are separated by the colon sign **:** which means either 'compared to' or 'compared with'.

For example, Jack has **one** sweet and Naomi has **two** sweets.

The ratio of sweets between Jack and Naomi is **1 : 2**, meaning Naomi has twice as many sweets as Jack.

1 : 2

The order of numbers in a ratio is important. Whichever item is mentioned first must come first in the ratio.

Example: | Kuldip has **£3** and Aaron has **£4**. Write the ratio of the amount of money they each have.

The coins' values below show how much money each child has. A colon separates the two amounts.

| Number of Parts Kuldip has | : | Number of Parts Aaron has |

£1 £1 £1 **:** £1 £1 £1 £1 **= 3 : 4**

Answer: **3 : 4**

Exercise 13: 1 Write the ratio for the amount:

Score

1) Akhil has **6** stickers and Adam has **7**. ____ : ____

2) Callum has **3** cakes and Ashish has **8**. ____ : ____

ae © 2016 Stephen Curran

25

3) Thaarini has **2cm** of ribbon and Jo has **9cm**. _____

4) Drashti has **3** pencils and Hadeeka has **5**. _____

5) Jaskirat's house has **2** bedrooms and Simran's has **3**. _____

6) Abbey has **6** sweets and Abhishek has **5**. _____

7) Barney has **£8** and Lloyd has **£11**. _____

8) Caleb has **5** apples and Martin has **3**. _____

9) Zeeshan has **5** pens and Kai has **7**. _____

10) William has **2** hats and Elzy has **7**. _____

2. Proportion

When both sides of a ratio are made smaller or larger by the same amount, the ratios are in **Proportion** to each other.

This is called scaling up and scaling down. Amounts that are scaled up or down are in proportion to one another.

For example, Georgie has **2** squares of chocolate and Sam has **4** squares of chocolate. They are in the ratio **2 : 4**.

These amounts can be scaled up (multipled by **2**) or scaled down (divided by **2**).

Scaled Down   **Original**   **Scaled Up**

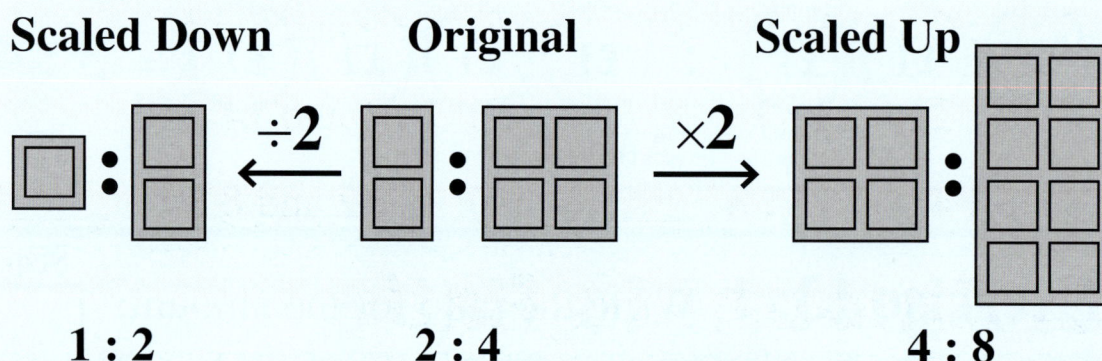

1 : 2   2 : 4   4 : 8

The squares of chocolate are **in proportion to each other** because Sam always has twice as many squares as Georgie.

Example: Is the ratio of **3 : 2** in proportion to **6 : 5**?

The ratios can be shown using apples and pears:

Apples : Pears
3 : 2

Apples : Pears
6 : 5

There are twice as many apples in the second ratio. If the ratio is multiplied by **2**, there should be **4** pears. However, the ratio contains **5** pears, so these ratios are not in proportion to each other.

$$3 : 2$$
$$\times 2 \downarrow$$
$$6 : 4$$

Answer: **No**

Exercise 13: 2

Are the ratios in proportion to each other?

Score

1) **3 : 4** and **6 : 7** _____   2) **2 : 1** and **6 : 3** _____

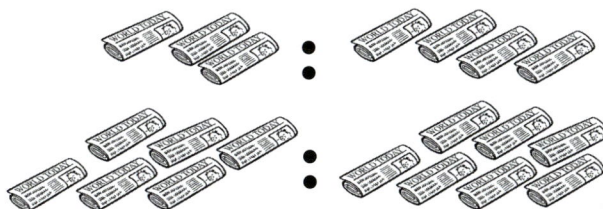

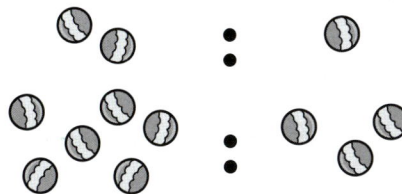

3) **7 : 3** and **14 : 4** _____   4) **8 : 6** and **4 : 3** _____

5) **6 : 2** and **12 : 4** _____   6) **8 : 9** and **1 : 3** _____

7) **4 : 2** and **2 : 1** _____   8) **7 : 6** and **14 : 10** _____

9) **5 : 4** and **15 : 8** _____   10) **16 : 2** and **8 : 1** _____

3. Amount to Ratio

Amounts can be converted to ratios in order to compare values. This involves showing the ratio in its simplest form.

Example: Express **£6** and **£8** as a ratio in lowest terms.

Step 1 - Insert a ratio colon between the two amounts.

$$£6 : £8$$

Step 2 - Simplify the amounts by dividing each side by **2**.

$$^{£3}\!\!\!\!\not{£6} : \not{£8}^{£4}$$

This ratio is now in its lowest terms.

$$£3 : £4$$

When simplifying, the ratios will always be in proportion to each other.

Answer: **£3 : £4**

Exercise 13: 3

Express the ratio in its lowest terms:

Score

1) **7m : 14m** _____   2) **6 : 2** _____

3) **£10 : £15** _____   4) **9 : 12** _____

5) **12 : 10** _____   6) **21 : 24** _____

7) **4p : 14p** _____   8) **8 : 36** _____

9) **18 : 10** _____   10) **16 : 20** _____

---

4. Ratio to Amount

In **Ratio to Amount** questions, a ratio and a total amount are given. The total amount must be divided up in proportion to the ratio to find an amount.

For example, there are **6** sweets and Phillip and Nancy eat them all.

Phillip eats twice as many as Nancy, in the ratio **2 : 1**. This means Phillip eats **4** sweets and Nancy eats **2** sweets.

$$2 : 1 = 3$$
$$\times 2$$
$$4 : 2 = 6$$

Example: Marbles are shared between Simran and Brahim in the ratio **2 : 3**. If there are **15** marbles in total, how many marbles does Brahim receive?

This type of question can be solved using a ratio box. Ratio boxes have four layers where information can be inserted: total, amounts, multiplier and ratio.

Step 1 - Insert the information given in the question into the ratio box. The ratio and total can be placed in the box.

Ratio - **2 : 3**
Total - **15**

Total
15
Amounts
? : ?
Multiplier
× ?
Ratio
2 : 3

Simran   Brahim

Step 2 - Add the two amounts in the ratio together.

2 + 3 = 5

Step 3 - Divide the total by **5**.

15 ÷ 5 = 3

This is the multiplier and can be placed in the box.

Total
15
Amounts
? : ?
Multiplier
× 3
Ratio
2 : 3

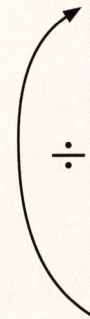

÷

2 + 3 = 5

Step 4 - Multiply the ratio by the multiplier to find the amounts.
2 × 3 = 6
3 × 3 = 9
The amounts are in proportion to the ratio and add up to the total of **15**.

Answer: **9**

Total
15
Amounts
6 : 9
Multiplier
× 3
Ratio
2 : 3

Remember the method has three operations:

Add   Divide   Multiply
+ → ÷ → ×

Exercise 13: 4   Find the amount:

1) Cakes are shared between Brad and Myriam in the ratio **3 : 4**. If there are **14** cakes in total, how many cakes does Brad receive? _____

Total
14
Amounts :
Multiplier ×
Ratio **3 : 4**

2) Building bricks are shared between Matthew and Will in the ratio **5 : 3**. If there are **24** bricks in total, how many bricks does Will receive? _____

Total
24
Amounts :
Multiplier ×
Ratio **5 : 3**

3) Felt pens are shared between Maneet and Kimran in the ratio **4 : 3**. If there are **21** pens in total, how many pens does Maneet receive? _____

PENS

Total
21
Amounts :
Multiplier ×
Ratio **4 : 3**

4) Lemonade is shared between Modesta and Lauren in the ratio **7 : 8**. If there are **150mℓ** in total, how much lemonade does Lauren receive? _____

Total
150mℓ
Amounts :
Multiplier ×
Ratio **7 : 8**

5) **£120** is shared between Cassie and Gemma in the ratio **7 : 3**. How much does Cassie receive? _____

Total
£120
Amounts :
Multiplier ×
Ratio **7 : 3**

6) **50cm** of ribbon is shared between Ana and Diana in the ratio **3 : 2**. How much does Diana receive? _____

Total
Amounts :
Multiplier ×
Ratio :

7) **55** seeds are shared out between Benjamin and Jasper in the ratio **6 : 5**. How many does Jasper receive? _____

Total	
Amounts :	
Multiplier ×	
Ratio :	

8) Mattias and Leon share **8** chalks between them in the ratio **3 : 1**. How many does Mattias receive? _____

Total	
Amounts :	
Multiplier ×	
Ratio :	

9) Biscuits are shared between Jolene and Rhys in the ratio **9 : 5**. If **28** are shared, how many does Jolene receive? _____

Total	
Amounts :	
Multiplier ×	
Ratio :	

10) Rachel and Kieran split a **100m** race between them in the ratio **3 : 7**. How far does Kieran have to run? _____

Total	
Amounts :	
Multiplier ×	
Ratio :	

5. Ratios & Fractions

Ratios can also be written as fractions.

For example, when making a cake, **4** cups of flour are mixed with **1** cup of sugar.

The ratio of flour to sugar is **4 : 1**.

There are **5** cups in total, so each cup is worth $\frac{1}{5}$ of the total.

Example: Russell buys **2** doughnuts and Katie buys **3** doughnuts. Write these amounts as a ratio and as fractions.

Step 1 - Write the ratio in the correct order: Russell first and Katie second. This is **2 : 3**.

Russell   **Katie**

Step 2 - Count the total number of parts.

$$2 + 3 = 5$$

The number **5** is the denominator, meaning each part is worth $\frac{1}{5}$.

Step 3 - As each part is worth $\frac{1}{5}$, Russell has $\frac{2}{5}$ and Katie has $\frac{3}{5}$.

Answer: **2 : 3**, $\frac{2}{5} : \frac{3}{5}$

Exercise 13: 5   Write the ratio for the amounts:

Score

1) Lianna owns **6** DVDs and Tobias owns **7**.

   $\underline{\ 6\ }$: $\underline{\ \ \ \ }$ $\frac{6}{13}$: $\frac{\ \ \ }{13}$

2) Payton owns **8** computer games and Nairmi owns **11**.

   $\underline{\ \ \ }$: $\underline{\ \ \ }$ $\frac{\ \ \ }{\ \ \ }$: $\frac{\ \ \ }{\ \ \ }$

3) **4** out of **9** boys like rugby, the others do not.

   $\underline{\ \ \ }$: $\underline{\ \ \ }$ $\frac{\ \ \ }{\ \ \ }$: $\frac{\ \ \ }{\ \ \ }$

4) **6** out of **11** pupils in a class are girls, the rest are boys.

____ : ____   — : —

5) Larry reads **7** books over the summer and Eden reads **5**.

____ : ____   — : —

6) **12** children have rabbits and **5** children have hamsters.

____ : ____   — : —

7) Thraen owns **7** CDs and Ash owns **8**.

____ : ____   — : —

8) **5** out of **12** children can ride a bike and the rest cannot.

____ : ____   — : —

9) Fergal owns **3** dogs and Melantha owns **2**.

____ : ____   — : —

10) Rhodri collects **12** apples and Graeme collects **11**.

____ : ____   — : —

6. Ratios & Percentages

Ratios can also be written as percentages. For example, **£1** is divided between Justin and Paula in the ratio **1 : 3**.

Justin would receive $\frac{1}{4}$ and Paula would receive $\frac{3}{4}$.

This means that as there are **100p** in **£1**, Justin would receive **25p** and Paula would receive **75p**. This could also be written as percentages: **25% : 75%**.

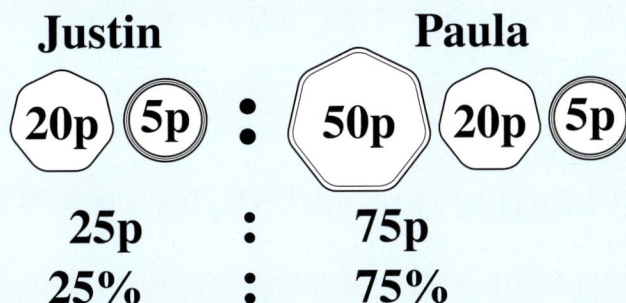

Justin	Paula
20p 5p :	50p 20p 5p
25p :	75p
25% :	75%

a. Ratio to Percentage

Example: | **20** books are shared between **2** children in the ratio **2 : 3**. Write the amounts received by each child as a percentage.

Step 1 - Write the ratio **2 : 3** as fractions. There are **5** parts in total, so each part is worth $\frac{1}{5}$.

$$\frac{2}{5} : \frac{3}{5}$$

Step 2 - Multiply each fraction by **100** to turn it into a percentage.

$$\frac{2}{\overset{1}{5}} \times \frac{\overset{20}{100}}{1} : \frac{3}{\overset{1}{5}} \times \frac{\overset{20}{100}}{1}$$

Step 3 - Cancel each side separately.   **40% : 60%**

Answer: **40% : 60%**

Exercise 13: 6

Write the percentages for the ratio:

Score

1) Oliver and Hannah share **500mℓ** of lemonade between them in the ratio **3 : 2**. ____ : ____

$$\frac{3}{5} \times \frac{100}{1} : \frac{2}{5} \times \frac{100}{1}$$

2) Eve and Charli share **25** chocolates in the ratio **2 : 3**.

____ : ____

3) **£10** is shared between Ritvar and Joel in the ratio

1 : 4. ____ : ____

Write the following shares as a ratio and as percentages:

4) Robyn has **one** dog and Shakira has **9** dogs.

____ : ____   ____ : ____

5) Saorise and Montague share **10** slices of pizza. Saorise eats **3** slices and Montague eats the rest.

____ : ____   ____ : ____

6) Sorana has **5** cakes. She gives **2** to Polly.

____ : ____   ____ : ____

7) Lewis is given **£50** and gives **£10** to Vee.

____ : ____   ____ : ____

8) Lizzy owns **4** CDs but loans **3** to Shelly.

____ : ____   ____ : ____

9) Tommy orders **4** drinks and gives **one** to Nesta.

____ : ____   ____ : ____

10) **Two** children share **one** cake and have **half** each.

____ : ____   ____ : ____

b. Percentage to Ratio

Example: | **20** books are shared between **2** children so that one receives **40%** and the other **60%**. Write the percentages as a ratio in its simplest form.

Step 1 - Write the percentages as a ratio.

40 : 60

Step 2 - Simplify the ratio by dividing by **20**.

$${}^{2}\cancel{40} : \cancel{60}^{3} = \boxed{2 : 3}$$

Answer: **2 : 3**

Exercise 13: 7

Write the percentage shares as a ratio:

1) **65% : 35%** = ____ : ____   2) **30% : 70%** = ____ : ____

3) **90% : 10%** = ____ : ____   4) **45% : 55%** = ____ : ____

5) Elle gets **75%** of the questions in her test correct. Write this as a ratio comparing the amount she got correct with the incorrect amount. ____ : ____

6) Rhiannon shared her cake with Luke so that she kept **60%** of it. Write this as a ratio. ____ : ____

7) **10** books are shared between **2** children so that one receives **10%** and the other receives the rest. Write this as a ratio. ____ : ____

8) Dave and Thierry are given **£20** and **£80** respectively. What are their shares as percentages and as a ratio?

____ : ____   ____ : ____

9) Danielle owns **7** out of **10** pairs of shoes and her sister owns the rest. What are their shares as percentages and as a ratio? ____ : ____   ____ : ____

10) Zac and Sky are given **30cm** and **20cm** of string respectively. What are their shares as percentages and as a ratio? ____ : ____   ____ : ____

7. Maps & Scale Drawings

Ratios are also used for **Maps & Scale Drawings**.
The actual distance represented on the map or scale drawing is in proportion to the ratio. A simpler form of the ratio box can be used.

a. Amount to Scale

Example: A classroom is **10m** in length. If a plan represents this as **5cm**, what is the scale?

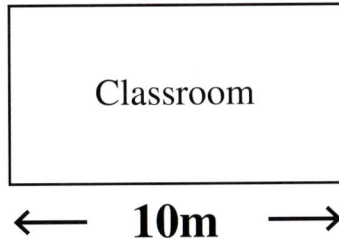

Classroom

$\longleftarrow$ **10m** $\longrightarrow$

Step 1 - Write the two amounts as a ratio.

5cm : 10m

Step 2 - Simplify the ratio, by dividing by **5**.

1cm : 2m

This is the scale.

Amounts
5cm : 10m
Divider
÷ 5
Scale
1cm : 2m

Answer: **1cm : 2m**

This can also be written using the same units.
This gives **1cm : 200cm** or simply **1 : 200**

Exercise 13: 8   Answer the following:

Score

1) A garden is **20m** in length. If a map shows this as **4cm**, what is the scale?
_____ : _____

Amounts
4cm : 20m
Divider
÷ 4
Scale
:

2) A living room of a house is **6** metres wide. If a plan represents this as **2cm**, what is the scale? _____ : _____

Amounts
2cm : 6m
Divider
÷
Scale
:

3) On a map, a mountain that is **4km** tall is shown as **2cm** tall. What is the scale? ____ : ____

Amounts
:
Divider
÷
Scale
:

4) A group of hikers plan a journey that is **6km** long. On a map this measures **2cm**. What is the scale? ____ : ____

Amounts
:
Divider
÷
Scale
:

5) A road measures **10m** in reality but on a map it is shown as **2cm**. What is the scale? ____ : ____

6) A bedroom is **4m** wide. If a plan shows this as **4cm**, what is the scale? ____ : ____

7) A scale drawing is made of a fridge freezer. The height on the drawing is **9cm** and the real height is **108cm**. What is the scale? ____ : ____

8) A plan is drawn for a wall. The wall measures **5cm** on the plan but is **1m** tall. What is the scale in centimetres? ____ : ____

9) A scale drawing is made of a table. The length of the table on the drawing is **4cm** and the real length is **1m 20cm**. What is the scale in centimetres? ____ : ____

10) A group of children do a cross-country run. Their run is **500m** long but measures **5cm** on the map. What is the scale in centimetres? ____ : ____

b. Scale to Amount

Example: On a plan a classroom is drawn at a scale of **1cm** to **2m**. If the length on the drawing is **5cm**, what is the actual length of the classroom?

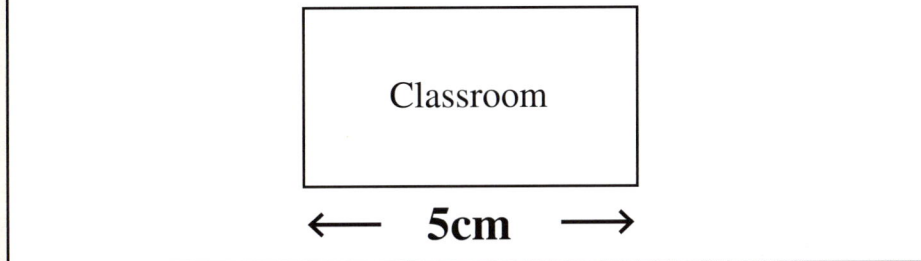

```
┌─────────────────────────┐
│                         │
│       Classroom         │
│                         │
└─────────────────────────┘
      ←──  5cm  ──→
```

Step 1 - Write out the ratio of the scale.

1cm : 2m

Step 2 - Find the multiplier by dividing **5** by **1**.
The multiplier is **5**.

Step 3 - Multiply the length on the plan by the multiplier.

$5 \times 2 = 10$

Answer: **10m**

Amounts
5cm : 10m
Multiplier
× 5
Scale
1cm : 2m

↑

Exercise 13: 9   Answer the following:

Score

1) A path around a pond is being tiled. The path is **10m** long. A plan was drawn using a scale of **1cm : 2m**. What does the path measure on the plan? _____

Amounts
: 10m
Multiplier
× 5
Scale
1cm : 2m

2) A ship sails a distance of **600km**. The scale of the map is **1cm** to **50km**. What does this measure on the map?

_____

Amounts
: 600km
Multiplier
× 12
Scale
1cm : 50km

3) A plan of a room is drawn to a scale of **2cm : 3m**. On the plan, the room is **6cm** long. What is the actual length? _____

| Amounts : |
| Multiplier × |
| Scale : |

4) A map of a city is drawn to a scale of **3cm : 15km**. How would **30km** be represented on the map? _____

| Amounts : |
| Multiplier × |
| Scale : |

5) A running track is drawn to a scale of **1cm : 150m**. The distance of one lap on the plan is **6cm**. What is the actual distance of one lap? _____

6) A map of France is drawn to a scale of **5cm : 10km**. What real distance is represented by **30cm**? _____

7) An aeroplane flies a distance of **650km**. On a map the scale is **1cm : 50km**. What does this measure on the map? _____

8) Alisha takes her dog for a walk around a lake. The path around the lake is drawn on a map using a scale of **1cm : 3km**. The distance measured on the map is **6cm**. What is the actual distance? _____

9) A plan of a room is drawn to a scale of **2cm : 5m**. The actual length of the room is **10m** long. What is the length on the plan? _____

10) The scale of a map is **2cm : 15km**. The journey a ship sails is represented by **10cm** on the map. What is the actual distance? _____

8. Problem Solving

Example: | Lily has **40** fish in her fish tank. **Two** out of every **five** fish are goldfish, the rest are minnows. How many goldfish are in Lily's fish tank?

This question can be solved using a ratio box.

Step 1 - Work out what **two** out of every **five** is as a ratio. The total number of parts is **5**. This means **2** parts of the **5** must be goldfish and **3** parts of the **5** must be minnows.

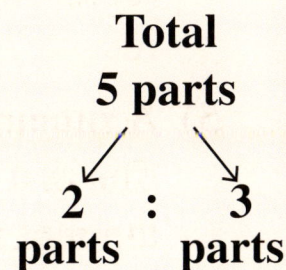

Total
5 parts

2 : 3
parts   parts

Step 2 - Insert the information given in the question into the ratio box. The ratio and the total can be placed in the box.

Ratio - **2 : 3**

Total - **40**

Step 3 - **Add** the two amounts in the ratio together.
$2 + 3 = 5$

Step 4 - **Divide** the total by **5**.
$40 \div 5 = 8$

This is the multiplier.

Total
40
Amounts
16 : 24
Multiplier
× 8
Ratio
2 : 3

Goldfish   Minnows

Step 5 - **Multiply** the ratio by the multiplier to find the amounts.
$2 \times 8 = 16$
$3 \times 8 = 24$

Answer: **16**

Exercise 13: 10 Answer the following:

1) Dom scores **7** out of **10** of the goals scored in a football tournament. Adam scores the rest. If **50** goals were scored over the whole tournament, how many did Adam score? _____

2) **48** mints are shared between Odin and Charlotte in the ratio **5 : 3**. How many mints does Charlotte receive? _____

3) Scott eats **75%** of the lunch he takes to school. Write this as a ratio comparing the amount eaten to the amount not eaten. _____

4) Myles has a set of **35** pens. **Three** out of every **seven** pens are blue and the rest are black. How many black pens does he have? _____

5) Trevor looks after cats. **Three** out of every **eight** are tabby cats and the rest are Bengal. If Trevor looks after **64** cats, how many are Bengal cats? _____

6) The ratio of boys to girls in a class is **3 : 4**. If there are a total of **21** children in the class, how many boys are in the class? _____

7) Kirsty owns **13** CDs and Nick owns **14**. Write this as a ratio. _____

8) Shane and Mitchell share **32** stickers in the ratio **1 : 3**. How many stickers does Shane receive? _____

9) Poppy and Noah receive **£80** to share in the ratio of **5 : 3**. How much does Poppy receive? _____

10) A map of the Isle of Lewis is drawn to a scale of **2cm : 3km**. How would **15km** be represented on the map? _____

Chapter Fourteen
PROBABILITY
1. What is Probability?

Probability is a way of measuring how **likely** something is to happen.

This happening is called an **event** or **outcome**. An event that has not yet happened is a **possibility**.

Some probabilities cannot be measured exactly. They can range from **definite (certain)** through to **impossible**, as in the following examples.

Certain	The sun will rise tomorrow.	
↑		
Likely	I will have three meals today.	
↑		
Possible	It will rain tomorrow.	
↑		
Unlikely	I will win the lottery jackpot.	
↑		
Impossible	I will fly to Mars next week.	

Example: | What is the probability that it will never rain again? Choose from the following options: certain   likely   possible   unlikely   impossible

Although there can be long periods of time when it does not rain, it is impossible that it will never rain again.

Answer: **impossible**

Exercise 14: 1 Write if the event is certain, likely, possible, unlikely or impossible:

1) If today is Saturday, tomorrow will be Sunday.

   _____

2) I will speak to a member of my family today.

   _____

3) There are **24** hours in a day. _____

4) Winter immediately follows summer. _____

5) It will rain tomorrow. _____

6) I will see the queen tomorrow. _____

7) I will eat ice-cream in summer. _____

8) Monday is followed by Thursday. _____

9) The Prime Minister will deliver a speech this week.

   _____

10) There will be an earthquake tomorrow. _____

2. Equal Probabilities

It is possible to exactly measure probability when all the possible results have the same chance of occurring. This means **all the probabilities are equal**.

Objects that give equal probabilities are described as **fair** as each outcome is equally likely.

This applies to objects such as dice, spinners, coins and playing cards.

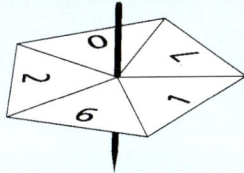

Dice	A Spinner	A Coin	Playing Cards
6 equal shaped sides. An equal chance of throwing a **1**, **2**, **3**, **4**, **5** or **6**.	5 equal shaped sides. Each face is equally likely to be landed on.	2 equal sides. An equal chance of tossing a head or a tail.	52 cards that look identical when face down. Choosing any card is equally likely.

An object is **unfair** or **biased** if it does **not** give equally likely outcomes.

Same coin

For example, a fake coin with tails on both sides would not be a fair coin.

Example: If these three cards are removed from a pack of playing cards, is it a 'fair' pack?

It is an unfair or biased pack because there is no longer an equal chance of selecting a card from a complete pack of **52** playing cards.

Answer: **No**

Exercise 14: 2

Does the event have equal probability? Write yes or no:

Score

1) A six-sided die with sides numbered **1**, **2**, **3**, **4**, **5** and **5**.

   _____

2) A complete pack of **52** playing cards. _____

3) A coin with **two** heads. _____

4) A spinner with **5** unequally sized sections. _____

5) A normal **6-sided** die. _____

Write whether the following are fair or unfair:

6) The toss of a coin where both heads and tails are equally likely. _____

7) A spinner with **6** equal sides. _____

8) A weighted die so that **one** number is more likely. _____

9) Picking a card from a complete set of **52** playing cards. _____ ♥ ♦ ♠ ♣

10) Picking a card from an incomplete set of **43** playing cards. _____

3. Possible Outcomes

An **Outcome** is the **result** of an activity or event.

For example, when a die is rolled, this is called the event. It can land on a **1, 2, 3, 4, 5** or **6** and these numbers are the **set of all possible outcomes**.

A set of all possible outcomes can be listed for any object that gives equal probabilities.

Example: What are all the possible outcomes if a **1p** coin is tossed?

A fair coin that is tossed fairly will only give two possible outcomes: **heads** or **tails**. This means that heads and tails is the set of all possible outcomes.

Answer: **heads and tails**

Exercise 14: 3

Write out the set of all possible outcomes:

1) Cards of **one** suit in a set of playing cards.

   ____ ____ ____ ____ ____ ____ ____

   ____ ____ ____ ____ ____ ____

2) A fair die. ____ ____ ____ ____ ____ ____

3) Tossing a fair coin. _____ _____

4) A spinner with **5** sides that are numbered from **1** to **5**.

   ____ ____ ____ ____ ____

5) A bag containing **four** different coloured balls: red, yellow, green and blue.

   _____ _____ _____ _____

6) The colours in a rainbow.

   _____ _____ _____ _____

   _____ _____ _____

7) A four-coloured pen: red, blue, black and green.

   _____ _____ _____ _____

8) A multiple-choice question with options A to E.

   ____ ____ ____ ____ ____

9) A spinner with **5** sides, with **4** sides that are numbered **1-4** and another side numbered **2**.

   ____ ____ ____ ____ ____

10) A spinner with odd and even numbers on it.

   _____ _____

4. Calculating Probability

Probabilities that can be exactly calculated can be written as fractions as follows:

$$P(\ ) = \frac{\text{Number of Favourable Outcomes}}{\text{Total Number of Possible Outcomes}}$$

- P is the symbol for probability.
- The name of the event is placed in the brackets ( ).
- The numerator of the fraction describes how many times the event could occur.
- The denominator describes how many possible outcomes there could be.

For example, the probability of tossing tails on a coin would be written as:

$$P(\text{tails}) = \frac{1}{2}$$

There are **two** possible outcomes (heads or tails); the denominator is **2**. Landing on tails can only occur **once**; the numerator is **1**.

This can also be written as a **1** in **2** chance.

Example: What is the probability of throwing an even number when rolling a die?

Step 1 - List the favourable outcomes; the even numbers.

      2, **4** or **6** (**three** in total)

Step 2 - List all of the possible outcomes.

      1, **2**, **3**, **4**, **5** or **6** (**six** in total)

Step 3 - Place these amounts into the fraction.

$$P(\ ) = \frac{\text{Number of Favourable Outcomes}}{\text{Total Number of Possible Outcomes}}$$

$$P(\text{even}) = \frac{3}{6}$$

'Even' is placed inside the brackets as this is the name of the event.

Step 4 - Simplify the fraction:

Divide by **3**

$$\frac{\cancel{3}^{\,1}}{\cancel{6}^{\,2}} = \frac{1}{2}$$

Answer: $P(\text{even}) = \frac{1}{2}$

or **a 1 in 2 chance**

Exercise 14: 4   Answer the following:

1) What is the probability of choosing a red sweet out of **seven** different coloured sweets?

   $P(\text{red}) = \underline{\ \ \frac{1}{7}\ \ }$ or a ___ in ___ chance

2) What is the probability of choosing the winning ticket out of **3** tickets?

   $P(\text{winning ticket}) = \underline{\ \ \ \ \ }$ or a _1_ in _3_ chance

3) What is the probability of tossing tails on a fair coin?

   $P(\text{tails}) = \underline{\ \ \ \ \ }$ or a ___ in ___ chance

4) What is the probability of picking the queen of spades out of a pack of **52** playing cards?

   $P(\text{one card}) = \underline{\ \ \ \ \ }$ or a ___ in ___ chance

5) What is the probability of rolling a **2** on a fair die?

   $P(\text{two}) = \underline{\ \ \ \ \ }$ or a ___ in ___ chance

6) What is the probability of landing on a **3** on a fair **5-sided** spinner?

   $P(\text{three}) = \underline{\ \ \ \ \ }$ or a ___ in ___ chance

---

The following questions need simplifying:

7) What is the probability of choosing a heart out of a pack of **52** playing cards (there are **4** suits, each of **13** cards)?

P(heart) = _____ or a ___ in ___ chance

8) If Tom buys **20** raffle tickets out of a total of **100** sold, what is his chance of winning first prize?

P(prize) = _____ or a ___ in ___ chance

9) What is the probability of throwing an even number when rolling a die?

P(even) = _____ or a ___ in ___ chance

10) In a bag of **3** blue, **4** red and **3** yellow balls, what is the probability of picking a red ball at random?

P(red) = _____ or a ___ in ___ chance

5. The Probability Scale

All probabilities can have a value between **zero** and **a whole one** (**0** to **1**).
This can be shown on the **Probability Scale**:

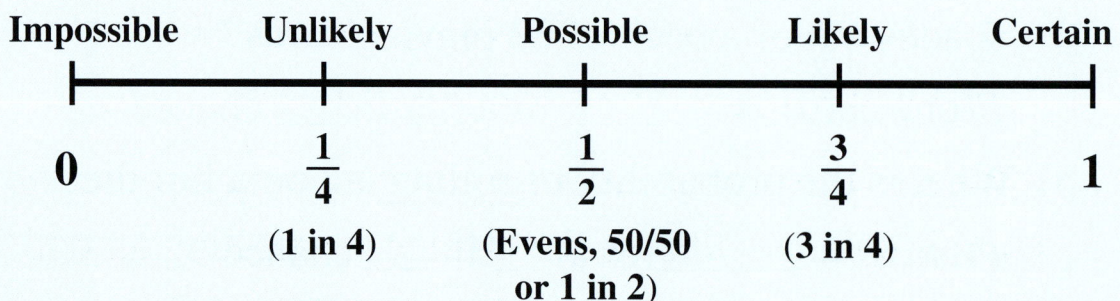

Impossible	Unlikely	Possible	Likely	Certain
0	$\frac{1}{4}$	$\frac{1}{2}$	$\frac{3}{4}$	**1**
	(**1 in 4**)	(**Evens, 50/50 or 1 in 2**)	(**3 in 4**)	

This means that the probability of all the possible outcomes of an event add up to or are equal to **1**.

Example: If there is a $\frac{1}{5}$ chance of landing on an odd number on a fair spinner, what is the chance of landing on an even number?

The total of all the possible outcomes must be **1**.

$$P(\textbf{odd}) + P(\textbf{even}) = 1$$

The probability of landing on an odd number is $\frac{1}{5}$, so:

$$\frac{1}{5} + P(\textbf{even}) = 1.$$

Subtract from **1** to find the probability of landing on an even number:

$$1 - \frac{1}{5} = \frac{4}{5}$$

Answer: $P(\textbf{even}) = \frac{4}{5}$

or **a 4 in 5 chance**

Score

Exercise 14: 5 Answer the following:

1) If there is a $\frac{1}{2}$ chance of throwing a heads on a coin, what is the chance a tails will be thrown? _____

2) If there is a $\frac{1}{3}$ chance of rolling a multiple of **3** on a die, what is the chance a multiple of **3** will not be rolled? _____

3) If there is a $\frac{3}{4}$ chance of picking a white ball, what is the chance a white ball will not be picked? _____

4) If there is a $\frac{3}{5}$ chance of spinning an even number on a fair spinner, what is the chance of spinning an odd number? _____

5) If there is a $\frac{1}{4}$ chance that a diamond will be picked, what is the chance a diamond will not be picked? _____

6) If there is a $\frac{3}{7}$ chance of picking a boy to read the story, what is the chance of picking a girl? _____

7) If there is a $\frac{9}{10}$ chance that a blue pen will be picked, what is the chance a blue pen will not be picked? _____

8) If there is a $\frac{1}{6}$ chance of being picked for the team, what is the chance of not being picked for the team? _____

9) If there is a $\frac{3}{8}$ chance of winning a prize, what is the chance of not winning a prize? _____

10) If there is a $\frac{1}{6}$ chance of rolling a **1** on a die, what is the chance of not rolling a **1**? _____

6. Expressing Probability

All probabilities have a value between **0** and **1** and can be expressed as **fractions**, **decimals** or **percentages**.
This can be shown on the probability scale.

Impossible	Unlikely	Possible	Likely	Certain
0	$\frac{1}{4}$	$\frac{1}{2}$	$\frac{3}{4}$	1
0	0.25	0.5	0.75	1
0	25%	50%	75%	100%

This also means that the probability of all the possible outcomes for an event add up to **1** (**one whole** or **100%**).

The total of the probabilities of all possible outcomes of an event is equal to 1.

Example: In a pack with **1** yellow, **7** orange and **2** red sweets, what is the probability of picking an orange sweet at random as a percentage?

Step 1 - Find the total possible outcomes.

1 yellow + **7** orange + **2** red = **10** sweets

Step 2 - Find the favourable outcomes; the orange sweets. There are **7** orange sweets.

Step 3 - Place these amounts into the fraction.

$$P(\text{orange}) = \frac{7}{10}$$

Step 4 - Convert the fraction to a percentage:

$$\frac{7}{10} = 70\%$$

Answer: **P(orange) = 70%**

Exercise 14: 6

Calculate the following, giving the answers as percentages:

Score

1) What is the probability of picking a brown felt-tip pen out of **10** different colours? _____

2) What is the probability of choosing a winning ticket out of **5** tickets? _____

3) In a pack of **5** black, **3** blue and **2** red pens, what is the probability of picking a red pen at random? _____

4) What is the probability of throwing an even number when rolling a die? _____

5) **One** sweet is picked at random from a bag containing **5** mints, **10** chews and **5** chocolates. What is the probability that a chocolate is not picked? _____

Calculate the following, giving the answers as decimals:

6) What is the probability of tossing heads on a coin? _____

7) What is the probability of picking a spade out of a pack of **52** playing cards (there are **4** suits, each of **13** cards)? _____

8) If Amy buys **20** raffle tickets out of a total of **50** sold, what is her chance of winning first prize? _____

9) A money box holds **5** twenty pence coins, **3** ten pence coins and **2** five pence coins. What is the probability of picking a ten pence coin at random? _____

10) In a pack of **4** blue pens and **1** red pen, what is the probability of picking a blue pen? _____

7. Problem Solving

Example: | **30** children place their names in a hat to be selected for class monitor. There are **18** boys and the rest are girls. What is the probability, as a decimal, that the monitor will be a girl?

Step 1 - Calculate how many girls are in the class.

30 − 18 = 12 girls

Step 2 - Place these amounts into the fraction and simplify.

Divide by **6**

$$P(\text{girl}) = \frac{12^{2}}{30^{5}} = \frac{2}{5}$$

Step 3 - Convert the fraction to a decimal: $\frac{2}{5} = 0.4$

Answer: **P(girl) = 0.4**

Exercise 14: 7   Answer the following:

1) There are **10** red balls, **5** green balls and **10** blue balls in a bag. What is the probability as a fraction of picking a green ball? _____

2) **One** card is drawn at random from an ordinary pack of **52** playing cards (there are **13** cards in each of the **4** suits). What is the probability as a fraction of drawing a queen? _____

3) **One** sweet is picked at random from a bag containing **3** chews, **5** chocolates and **5** mints. What is the probability as a fraction of picking a chew? _____

4) If there is a $\frac{4}{5}$ chance of picking a winning ticket, what is the probability a winning ticket will not be picked? Give the answer as a percentage. _____

5) In a class of **10** boys and **15** girls, what is the chance as a fraction of the teacher picking a boy at random? _____

6) If **10** raffle tickets are bought by one person out of a total of **100**, what is the chance as a fraction of them winning first prize? _____

7) A child wants to roll a **6** using a fair die. What is the probability as a fraction of rolling a **6**? _____

8) A spinner has **2** green sections, **1** white section, **1** red section and **1** blue section. What is the probability as a fraction of the spinner landing on a green section? _____

9) In a packet of **20** sweets, there are **14** that a child likes. What is the probability as a fraction of the child picking a sweet they like? _____

10) Only a number that ends in a **0** or a **5** can win the tombola. In **100** tickets, only **20** win a prize. What is the probability that Akhil picks a ticket that does not win? Give the answer as a decimal. _____

Chapter Fifteen
LINES & ANGLES
1. Types of Line

A **Line** joins two points together. Lines can be straight or curved, as shown below:

Straight   **Curved**

Lines can be described in the following ways:

Horizontal • Vertical • Diagonal
Parallel • Perpendicular

Vertical Lines

A line drawn straight 'up' or 'down' or exactly upright.

Horizontal Lines

A line drawn straight 'across' flat like the horizon.

Diagonal Lines

A straight line that slants is a **diagonal**. Any straight line that is not horizontal or vertical is diagonal.

Parallel Lines

Lines that always stay the same distance apart and never meet are **parallel**.

Arrows can be used to show the lines are parallel. Parallel lines can be straight or curved.

Perpendicular Lines

When a horizontal line meets a vertical line the two lines are **perpendicular** to each other. If these two lines are turned they are still perpendicular to each other.

Example: Complete the following:
The rungs of a ladder are _____ to each other. (perpendicular, horizontal, parallel)

The rungs remain the same distance apart and never meet. This means they are parallel to each other.

Answer: **parallel**

Exercise 15: 1   Answer the following:

Score

1) Train tracks are _____ to each other. (horizontal, parallel, perpendicular)

2) The legs of a chair are _____ to each other. (perpendicular, vertical, parallel)

3) The legs of a table are _____ to the top of a table. (perpendicular, horizontal, parallel)

4) The walls of a room are _____. (diagonal, vertical, horizontal)

5) Two sides of a rhombus are _____. (diagonal, curved, perpendicular)

6) How many diagonal lines does this drawing have?

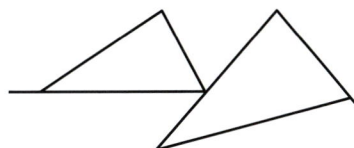

_____

7) How many vertical lines are there in this drawing?

_____

8) How many horizontal lines are there in this drawing?

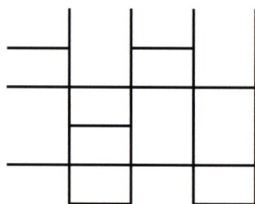

_____

9) How many diagonal lines are there in this drawing?

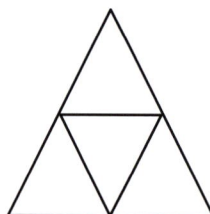

_____

10) How many vertical lines does this shape have?

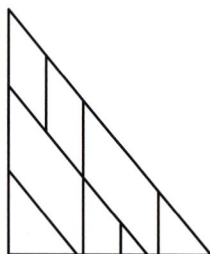

_____

2. Types of Angle

Angles are formed when two straight lines meet.

Angles are measured in degrees.

The degrees symbol is °.

A curved line is often used between the two straight lines to show an angle.

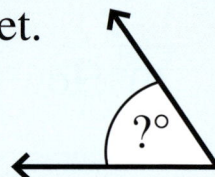

a. Right Angles & Straight Lines

A right angle equals **90°** and is the same as the corner of a square, rectangle or piece of paper. It is shown using a box symbol in the corner of the angle, like this: ⌐

A straight line equals **180°** and is formed from two right angles.

Right Angle
90°

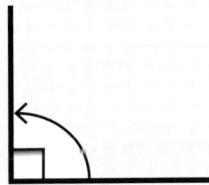

Straight Line
180°

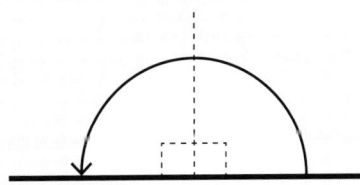

The diagrams show a line as it turns through **4** right angles to complete a full turn of **360°**.

A $\frac{1}{4}$ turn
90°

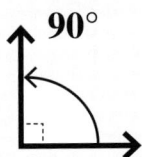

1 right angle

A $\frac{1}{2}$ turn
180°

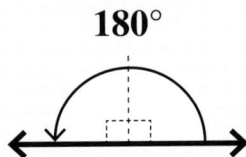

2 right angles

A $\frac{3}{4}$ turn
270°

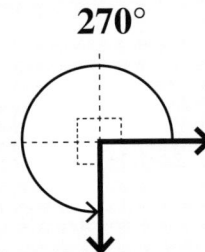

3 right angles

A full turn
360°

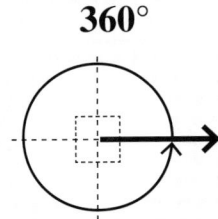

4 right angles

Right-hand turns are **Clockwise** (the direction in which the hands of a clock move) and left-hand turns are **Anticlockwise**.

Clockwise

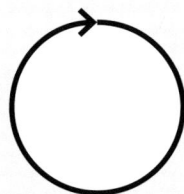

Anticlockwise

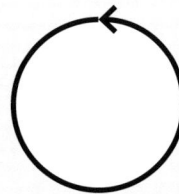

A useful way to remember clockwise and anticlockwise is that bottle tops are tightened clockwise and loosened anticlockwise.

Example: Is this angle a right angle?

If this angle is compared with a right angle, it is easy to see that it is less than **90°**.

Example Angle   Right Angle

Answer: **No**

Exercise 15: 2   Answer the following:

a    b 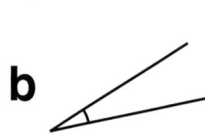   c 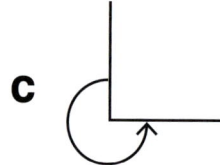   d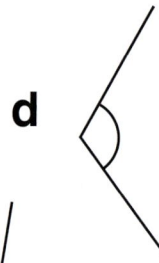

e 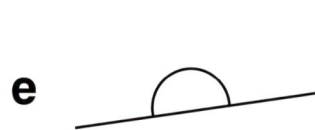   f 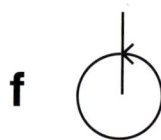   g 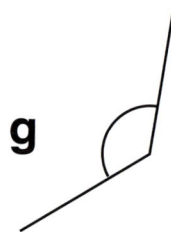   h

i 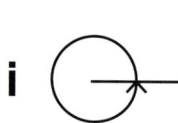   j

1) Which two angles show a $\frac{1}{4}$ turn? ____ ____

2) Is **b** a right angle? ____

3) Which two angles show a full turn? ____ ____

4) Which two angles are straight lines? ____ ____

5) Is **d** a right angle? ____

6) How many right angles are in **f**? ____

7) How many **90°** turns are in **i**? ____

8) Is **g** a right angle? ____

9) How many right angles are in **c**? ____

10) Is **j** a right angle? ____

b. Acute, Obtuse & Reflex Angles

Angles that are not right angles or straight lines can be split into three types:

      1. Acute   **2. Obtuse**   **3. Reflex**

Acute angles can be called 'narrow' angles and obtuse and reflex angles can be called 'wide' angles.

1. Acute - Up to 90°

An acute angle is any angle that is less than **90°**.

2. Obtuse - Above 90° to 180°

An obtuse angle is bigger than **90°** but less than **180°**.

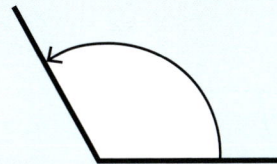

3. Reflex - Above 180° to 360°

A reflex angle is bigger than **180°** but less than **360°**. These angles are both reflex angles but look very different from each other.

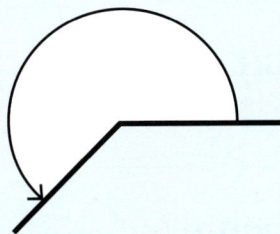

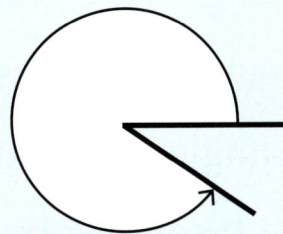

Example: | Is this wide angle obtuse or reflex?

If this angle is compared with a straight line, it is easy to see that it is more than **180°** and is reflex.

Example Angle   **Straight Line**

Answer: **reflex**

Exercise 15: 3   Answer the following:

a 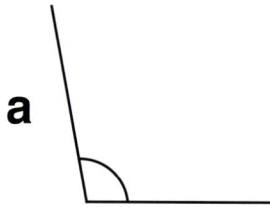   b 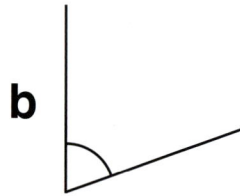   c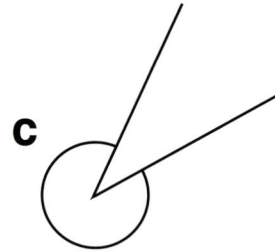

d 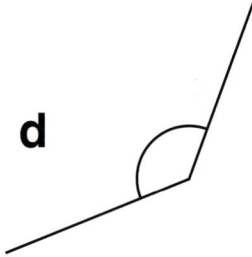   e 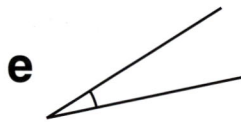   f 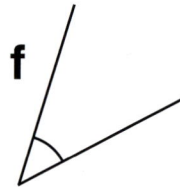   g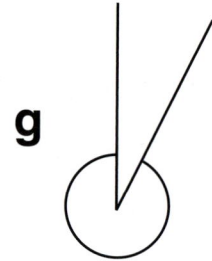

h 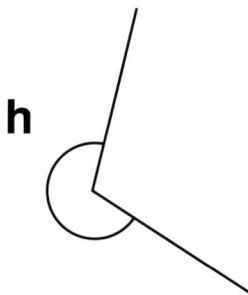   i 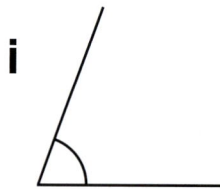   j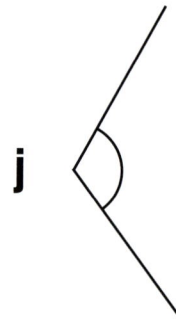

1) Which angles are greater than **180°**? _____

2) Which angles are less than **90°**? _____

3) Which angles are obtuse? _____

4) Is angle **b** reflex, obtuse or acute? _____

5) Is angle **d** reflex, obtuse or acute? _____

6) Is angle **h** reflex, obtuse or acute? _____

7) Is angle **f** reflex, obtuse or acute? _____

8) Is angle **i** reflex, obtuse or acute? _____

9) Is angle **c** reflex, obtuse or acute? _____

10) Is angle **j** reflex, obtuse or acute? _____

3. Line & Angle Relationships

When two angles are joined together they can form right angles, straight lines or full circles. These combined angles can have the following names:

Complementary • Supplementary • Conjugate

When two or more angles appear in the same diagram, angle relationships can be formed. Two of the most common are:

Adjacent • Opposite

Angles are not always drawn to scale or accurately drawn in questions. It is always important to use the given number of degrees in the question to find an answer.

a. Complementary Angles

Complementary Angles are two angles that together measure **90°** or a right angle. Angles *a* and *b* together make **90°**.

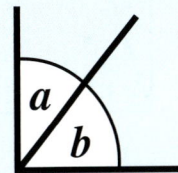

Example: What is the value of the complementary angle *a*?

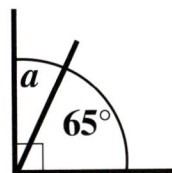

The two angles must add up to **90°** as they are complementary angles.

Subtract the given angle from the total to find the missing angle.

$$90° - 65° = 25°$$
Answer: **25°**

Exercise 15: 4a

Match up the complementary angles:

1)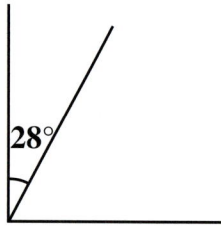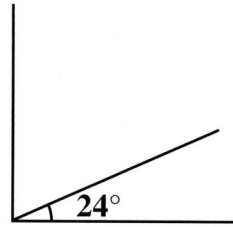

2)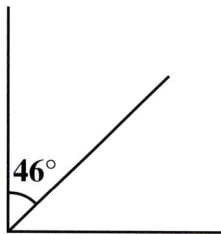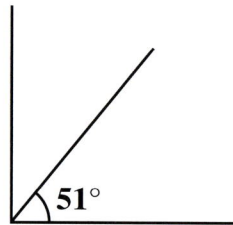

3)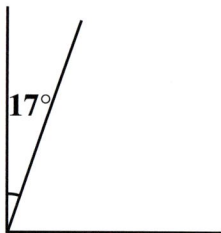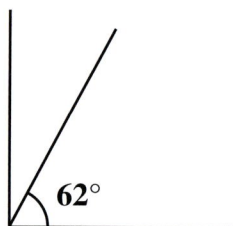

4)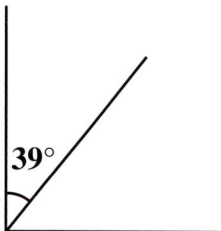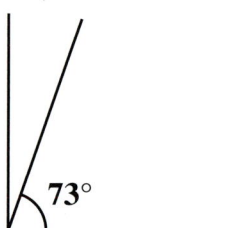

5)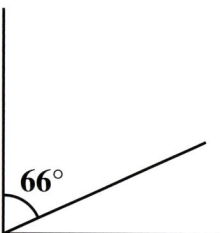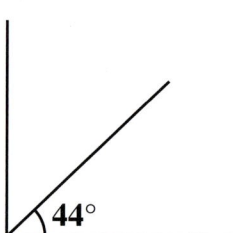

b. Supplementary Angles

Supplementary Angles are two angles that together measure **180°** or a straight line. Angles a and b together make **180°**.

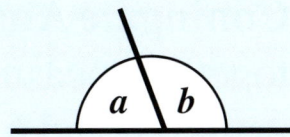

Example: What is the value of the supplementary angle a?

$133°$ a

The two angles must add up to **180°** as they are supplementary angles. Subtract to find the missing angle.

$$180° - 133° = 47°$$

Answer: **47°**

Exercise 15: 4b Match up the supplementary angles:

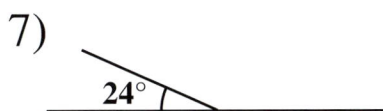

6) $105°$

7) $24°$

8) $97°$

9) $40°$

10) $132°$

$156°$

$140°$

$48°$

$83°$

$75°$

c. Conjugate Angles

Conjugate Angles are two angles that together measure **360°** or a full circle. Angles *a* and *b* together make **360°**.

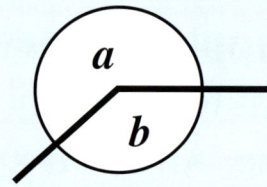

Example: What is the value of the conjugate angle *a*?

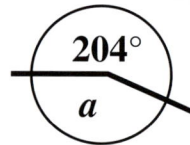

The two angles must add up to **360°** as they are conjugate angles. Subtract to find the missing angle.

$$360° - 204° = 156°$$

Answer: **156°**

Exercise 15: 5a

Match up the conjugate angles:

Score

1)   126°

2)   152°

3)   170°

4)   13°

5)   64°

190°

296°

208°

234°

347°

d. Opposite & Adjacent Angles

Angle relationships can be formed when angles are placed next to each other or when two or more lines cut across each other, which means the lines **intersect**.

Intersecting lines can form both opposite and adjacent angles.

Opposite

Opposite angles face each other across intersecting lines and are exactly the same size, as shown below:

$a = d$ and $b = c$
a & d and b & c
  are opposite.

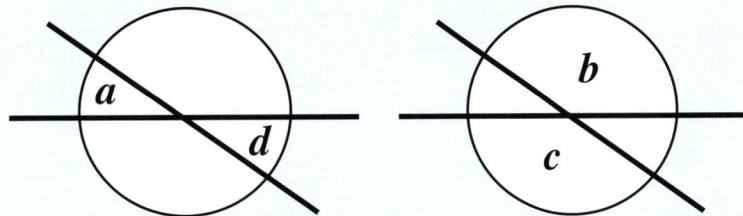

Adjacent

Adjacent angles are next to or beside each other across these intersecting lines, as shown below:

a & b, b & d, d & c and c & a are adjacent.

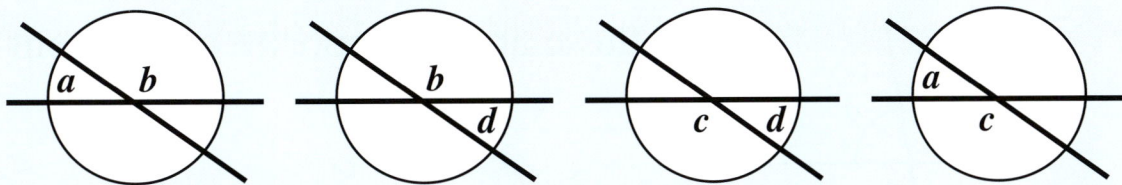

Example: Are angles a and b opposite or adjacent?

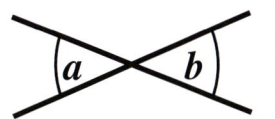

The two angles face each other and are exactly the same size. This means they are opposite angles.

Answer: **opposite**

Exercise 15: 5b Answer the following:

6)

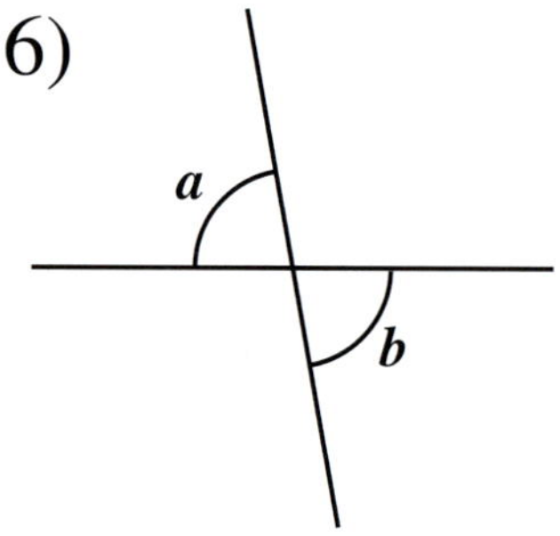

Are these angles opposite or adjacent?

_____

7)

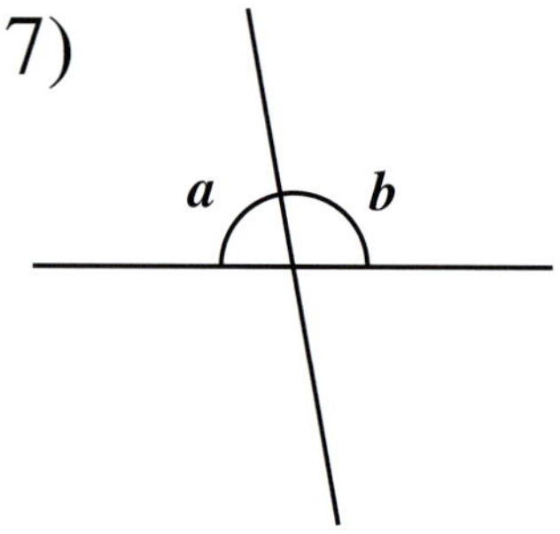

Are these angles opposite or adjacent?

_____

8)

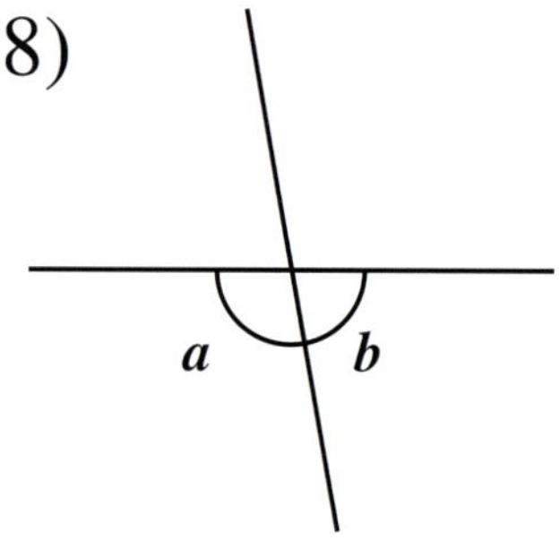

Are these angles opposite or adjacent?

_____

9)

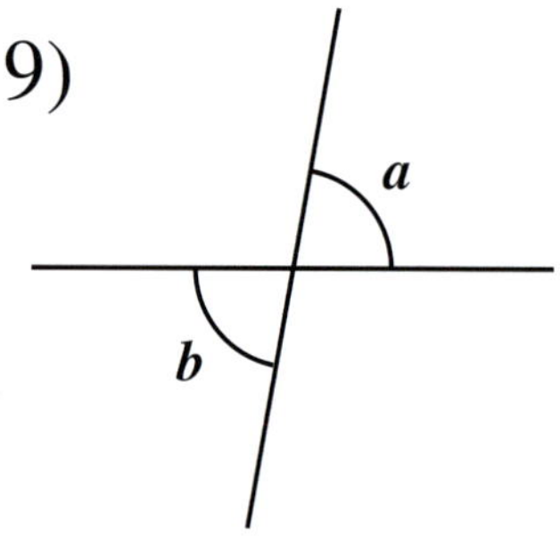

Are these angles opposite or adjacent?

_____

10)

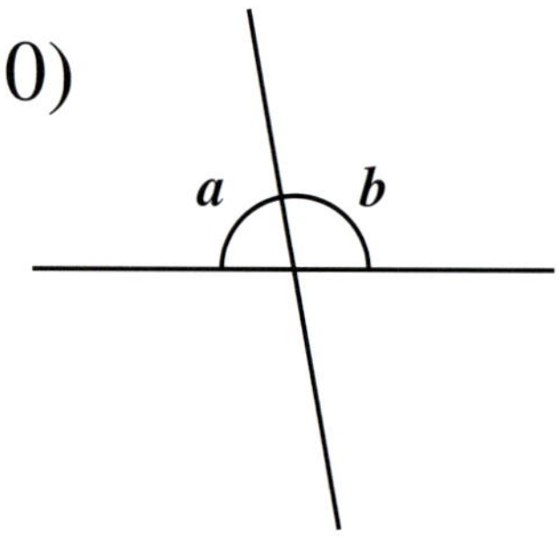

Are these angles adjacent to each other?

_____

e. Mixed Line & Angle Questions

Exercise 15: 6 Write the missing angle and line/angle relationship:

1)

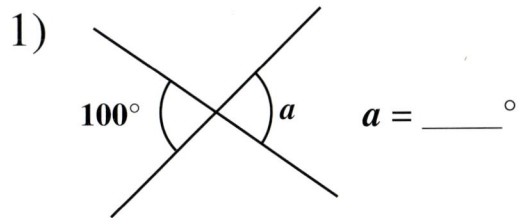

$a =$ _____ $^\circ$

_____ angle

2)

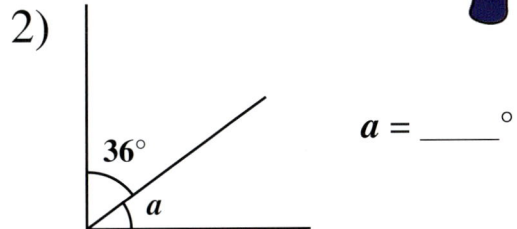

$a =$ _____ $^\circ$

_____ angle

3)

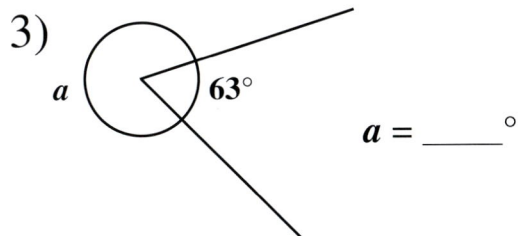

$a =$ _____ $^\circ$

_____ angle

4)

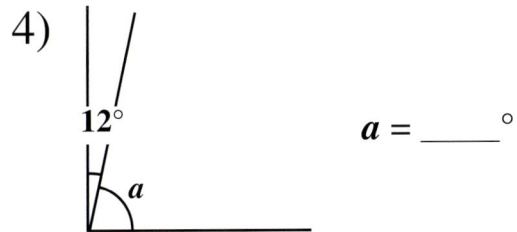

$a =$ _____ $^\circ$

_____ angle

5)

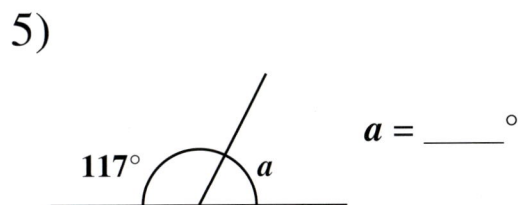

$a =$ _____ $^\circ$

_____ angle

6)

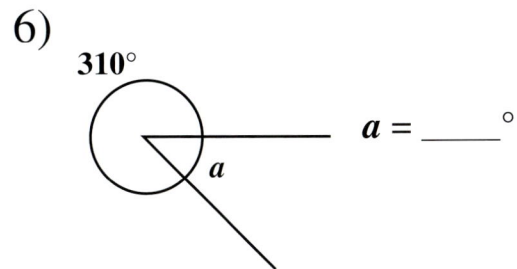

$a =$ _____ $^\circ$

_____ angle

7)

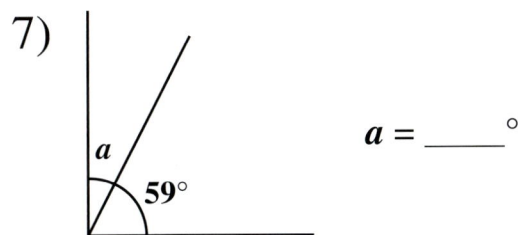

$a =$ _____ $^\circ$

_____ angle

8)

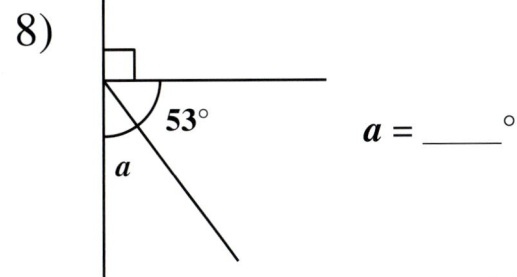

$a =$ _____ $^\circ$

_____ angle

9)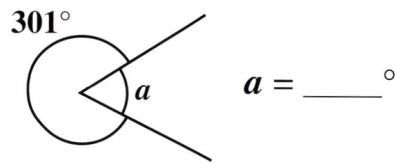

$a =$ _____ °

_____ angle

10)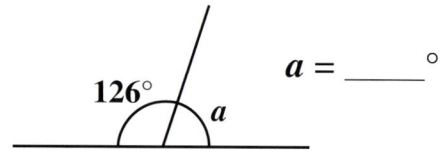

$a =$ _____ °

_____ angle

4. Measuring Angles

A **Protractor** is used to measure the size of an angle.

Protractors can be used to measure or draw angles to within **1°**, so they need to be used with care.

Use a sharp pencil to draw and mark angles.

This obtuse angle measures **125°**.

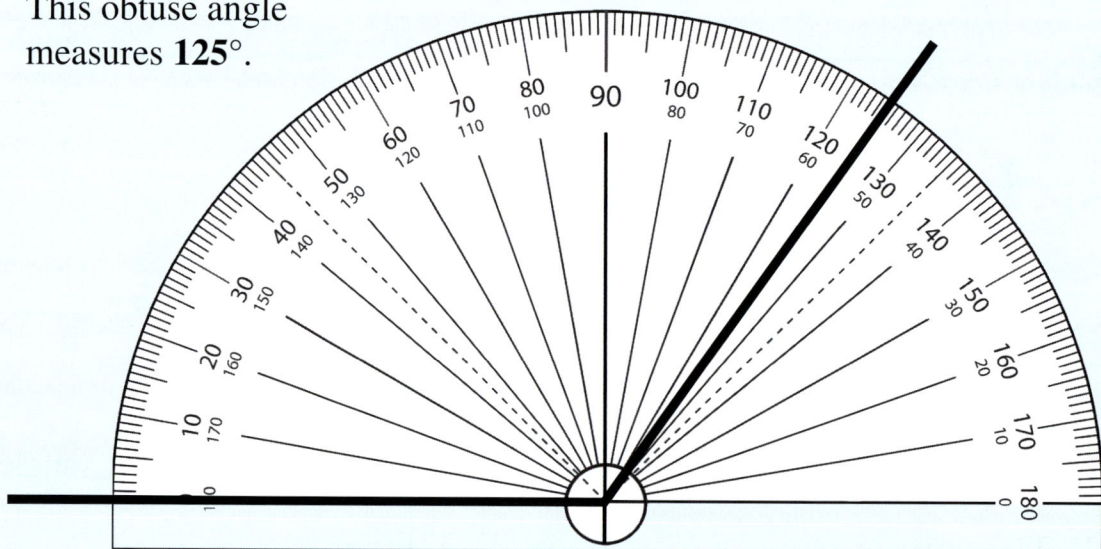

The protractor should be placed at the **bottom edge** or **0°** on the line to be measured.

The protractor has an inside and an outside scale so an angle can be measured from both sides. Make sure the angle is measured from the correct side (starting at **0°**).

Example: Measure this angle using a protractor.

Step 1 - This angle is acute and less than **90°**. Line up the bottom of the angle with the protractor's horizontal line of **0°**.

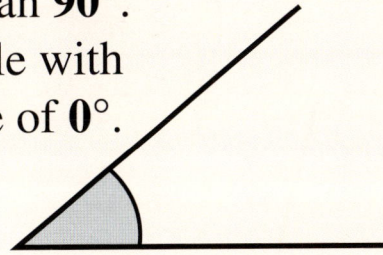

Step 2 - Use the inside scale to measure the angle in an anticlockwise direction.

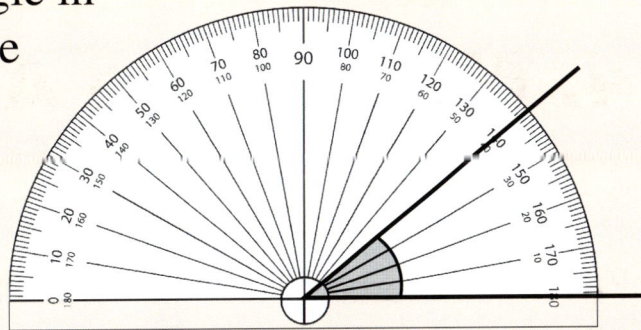

Step 3 - This angle measures **40°**.

Answer: **40°**

Exercise 15: 7

Calculate the angle using a protractor:

1) This angle is _____ .

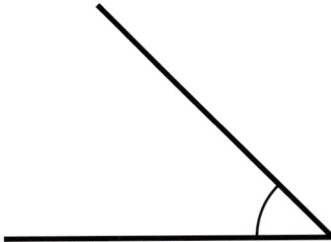

2) This angle is _____ .

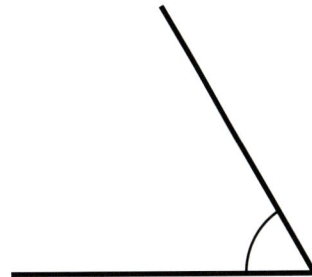

3) This angle is _____ .

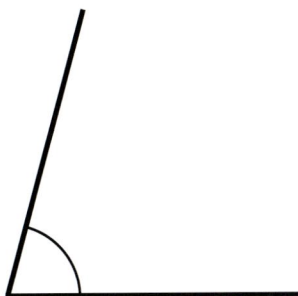

4) This angle is _____ .

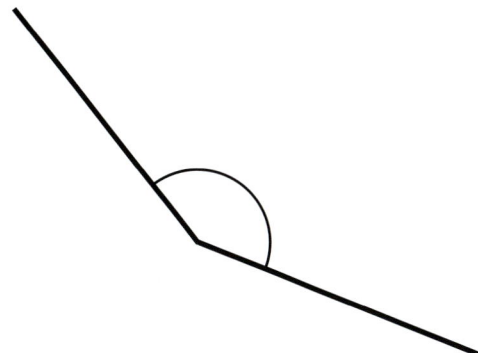

5) This angle is _____ .

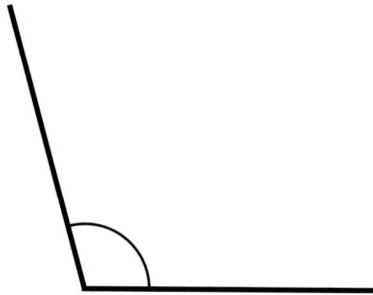

6) This angle is _____ .

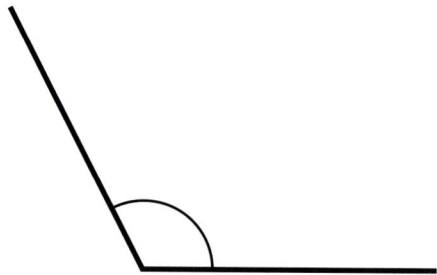

7) This angle is _____ .

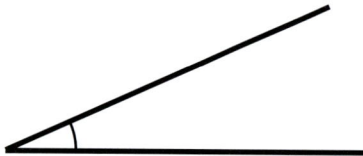

8) This angle is _____ .

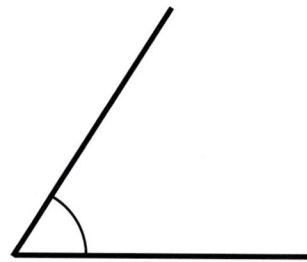

9) This angle is _____ .

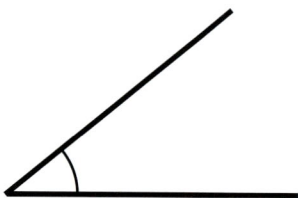

10) This angle is _____ .

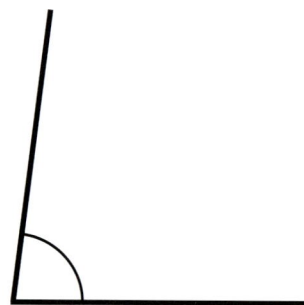

5. Bearings & Directions
a. The Compass

A **Compass** is an instrument that is used to calculate direction. The needle of a compass is magnetic and will always point north. All other directions can be found by measuring from north.

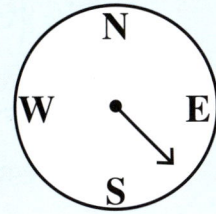

When angles are used to show direction they are called **Bearings**. Bearings are always measured from north.

There are eight main **Compass Directions**.

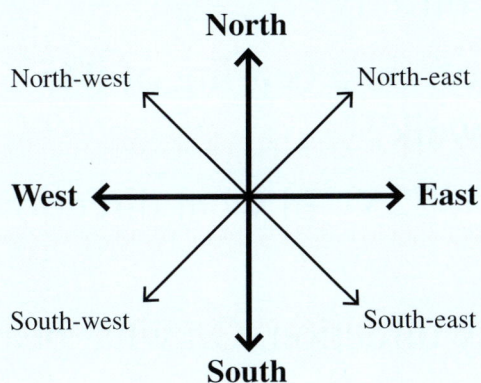

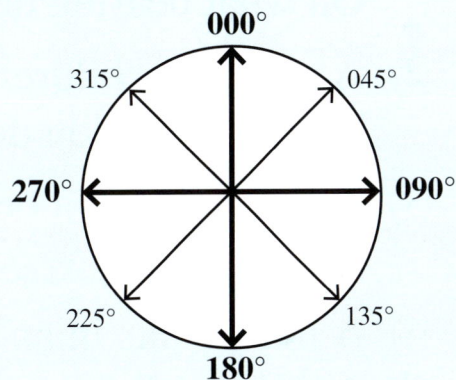

- The eight points of the compass can be measured in degrees, e.g. **270°** is west.
- Bearings are written in degrees as three figures, e.g. **060°**.
- Bearings are measured clockwise from the **north line**.
- A full turn of the compass is four right angles.

b. Finding a Bearing

Examples: | A ship sails in a south-west direction. What is the compass bearing?

Using the main compass points, a ship sailing south-west will be moving on a bearing of **225°**.

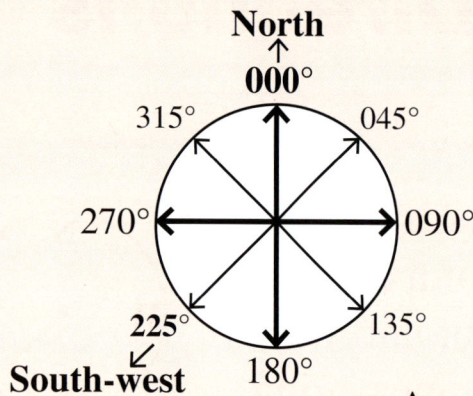

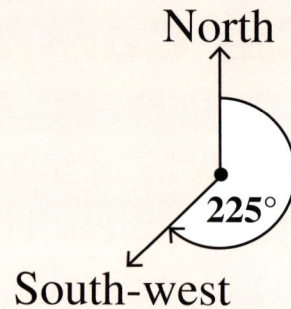

North
↑
000°
315°   045°
270°   090°
225°   135°
180°
South-west

North
↑
225°
South-west

Answer: **225°**

Exercise 15: 8 Answer the following:

1) A bird flies in a north-westerly direction. On what bearing does the bird fly? _____°

2) A group of children head off on a bearing of **045°**. In what direction do they walk? _____

3) A ship sails on a bearing of **225°**. In what direction is it sailing? _____

4) A man walks in an easterly direction. On what bearing does he walk? _____°

5) An aeroplane flies in a south-westerly direction. On what bearing does it fly? _____°

6) The shop is south of Paula's house. On what bearing would she need to walk to reach it? _____°

7) A ship sails in a north-easterly direction. On what bearing does it sail? _____°

8) Joshua walks on a bearing of **135°**. In which direction is he walking? _____

9) An athlete throws a javelin on a bearing of **090°**. In which direction is the javelin thrown? _____

10) An aeroplane takes off on a bearing of **180°**. In what direction is it heading? _____

Answers

Chapter Twelve
Percentages

Exercise 12: 1
1) 17%
2) 65%
3) 93%
4) 72%
5) Shade 51 squares
6) Shade 48 squares
7) Shade 39 squares
8) Shade 22 squares
9) 36%
10) 20% or other appropriate answer

Exercise 12: 2
1) $1/4$ 2) 60%
3) 70%   4) $1/2$
5) $1/5$ 6) 30%
7) $3/4$ 8) 90%
9) $2/5$ 10) 10%

Exercise 12: 3
1) $1/2$ 2) $1/4$
3) $13/20$ 4) $14/25$
5) $4/25$ 6) $47/50$
7) $19/50$ 8) $19/25$
9) $9/20$ 10) $4/5$

Exercise 12: 4
1) 48%   2) 60%
3) 90%   4) 70%
5) 34%   6) 32%
7) 55%   8) 54%
9) 16%   10) 82%

Exercise 12: 5
1) 0.27   2) 0.45
3) 0.07   4) 0.79
5) 0.39   6) 0.42
7) 0.16   8) 0.68
9) 0.12   10) 0.3

Exercise 12: 6
1) 1%   2) 25%
3) 56%   4) 80%
5) 93%   6) 14%
7) 37%   8) 62%
9) 48%   10) 79%

Exercise 12: 7
1) $1/10$ = 0.1 = 10%
2) $1/2$ = 0.5 = 50%
3) $5/5$ = 1 = 100%
4) $3/10$ = 0.3 = 30%
5) $3/4$ = 0.75 = 75%
6) $7/10$ = 0.70 = 70%
7) $9/10$ = 0.9 = 90%
8) $2/5$ = 0.4 = 40%
9) $3/5$ = 0.6 = 60%
10) $1/5$ = 0.2 = 20%

Exercise 12: 8
1) $1/10$, 0.11, 13%
2) 81%, $4/5$, 0.77
3) 0.15   4) $3/10$
5) 0.56   6) 42%
7) 0.26   8) 0.29
9) 71%   10) 5%

Exercise 12: 9
1) 30   2) 40
3) 3p   4) £1.30
5) 5.5   6) 3
7) 45kg   8) 27.5
9) 5g   10) 400

Exercise 12: 10
1) 224   2) 180
3) 1p   4) £23.40
5) 46.5   6) 405
7) 360kg   8) 560
9) 6g   10) 67.5

Exercise 12: 11
1) £36

2) 34
3) 186
4) 96cm
5) 72
6) 17
7) 49p
8) 63km
9) 81m
10) 276

Exercise 12: 12
1) 517
2) 606p
3) 1,230
4) 450
5) 189
6) £717.50
7) 71.5cm
8) 1,120
9) £262.50
10) 127.3m

Exercise 12: 13
1) 500
2) 51
3) £411.30
4) 490
5) 160cm
6) £166.60
7) 123
8) 540
9) 288
10) 652.41m

Exercise 12: 14
1) 50%
2) 25%
3) 25%
4) 42%
5) 6%
6) 20%
7) 10%

Answers

8) 16%
9) 1%
10) 25%

Exercise 12: 15
1) 28
2) 34
3) 25
4) 24.8km
5) 195
6) 8%
7) 13%
8) 20%
9) 45%
10) 9%

Exercise 12: 16
1) 6
2) 40%
3) £100
4) £4.40
5) 7
6) 117
7) 75%
8) 30%
9) 24
10) 70%

Chapter Thirteen
Ratio
Exercise 13: 1
1) 6 : 7
2) 3 : 8
3) 2cm : 9cm
4) 3 : 5
5) 2 : 3
6) 6 : 5
7) £8 : £11
8) 5 : 3
9) 5 : 7
10) 2 : 7

Exercise 13: 2
1) No   2) Yes
3) No   4) Yes
5) Yes   6) No
7) Yes   8) No
9) No   10) Yes

Exercise 13: 3
1) 1m : 2m   2) 3 : 1
3) £2 : £3   4) 3 : 4
5) 6 : 5   6) 7 : 8
7) 2p : 7p   8) 2 : 9
9) 9 : 5   10) 4 : 5

Exercise 13: 4
1) 6   2) 9
3) 12   4) 80mℓ
5) £84   6) 20cm
7) 25   8) 6
9) 18   10) 70m

Exercise 13: 5
1) 6 : 7, $^6/_{13}$: $^7/_{13}$
2) 8 : 11, $^8/_{19}$: $^{11}/_{19}$
3) 4 : 5, $^4/_9$: $^5/_9$
4) 6 : 5, $^6/_{11}$: $^5/_{11}$
5) 7 : 5, $^7/_{12}$: $^5/_{12}$
6) 12 : 5, $^{12}/_{17}$: $^5/_{17}$
7) 7 : 8, $^7/_{15}$: $^8/_{15}$
8) 5 : 7, $^5/_{12}$: $^7/_{12}$
9) 3 : 2, $^3/_5$: $^2/_5$
10) 12 : 11, $^{12}/_{23}$: $^{11}/_{23}$

Exercise 13: 6
1) 60% : 40%
2) 40% : 60%
3) 20% : 80%
4) 1 : 9, 10% : 90%
5) 3 : 7, 30% : 70%
6) 3 : 2, 60% : 40%
7) 4 : 1, 80% : 20%
8) 1 : 3, 25% : 75%

9) 3 : 1, 75% : 25%
10) 1 : 1, 50% : 50%

Exercise 13: 7
1) 13 : 7 2) 3 : 7
3) 9 : 1   4) 9 : 11
5) 3 : 1   6) 3 : 2
7) 1 : 9
8) 20% : 80%, 1 : 4
9) 70% : 30%, 7 : 3
10) 60% : 40%, 3 : 2

Exercise 13: 8
1) 1cm : 5m
2) 1cm : 3m
3) 1cm : 2km
4) 1cm : 3km
5) 1cm : 5m
6) 1cm : 1m
7) 1cm : 12cm
8) 1cm : 20cm
9) 1cm : 30cm
10) 1cm : 10,000cm

Exercise 13: 9
1) 5cm   2) 12cm
3) 9m   4) 6cm
5) 900m   6) 60km
7) 13cm   8) 18km
9) 4cm   10) 75km

Exercise 13: 10
1) 15   2) 18
3) 3 : 1   4) 20
5) 40   6) 9
7) 13 : 14 8) 8
9) £50   10) 10cm

Chapter Fourteen
Probability
Exercise 14: 1
1) Certain

Answers

*Key Stage 2 Maths
Year 4/5 Workbook 6*

2) Likely
3) Certain
4) Impossible
5) Possible
6) Unlikely
7) Likely
8) Impossible
9) Possible
10) Unlikely

Exercise 14: 2
1) No   2) Yes
3) No   4) No
5) Yes   6) Fair
7) Fair   8) Unfair
9) Fair   10) Unfair

Exercise 14: 3
1) Ace; 2; 3; 4; 5; 6;
   7; 8; 9; 10; Jack;
   Queen; King
2) 1; 2; 3; 4; 5; 6
3) heads; tails
4) 1; 2; 3; 4; 5
5) red; yellow; green; blue
6) red; orange; yellow;
   green; blue; indigo;
   violet
7) red; blue; black; green
8) A; B; C; D; E
9) 1; 2; 3; 4
10) odd; even

Exercise 14: 4
1) $^1/_7$ or a 1 in 7 chance
2) $^1/_3$ or a 1 in 3 chance
3) $^1/_2$ or a 1 in 2 chance
4) $^1/_{52}$ or a 1 in 52 chance
5) $^1/_6$ or a 1 in 6 chance
6) $^1/_5$ or a 1 in 5 chance

7) $^1/_4$ or a 1 in 4 chance
8) $^1/_5$ or a 1 in 5 chance
9) $^1/_2$ or a 1 in 2 chance
10) $^2/_5$ or a 2 in 5 chance

Exercise 14: 5
1) $^1/_2$ or a 1 in 2 chance
2) $^2/_3$ or a 2 in 3 chance
3) $^1/_4$ or a 1 in 4 chance
4) $^2/_5$ or a 2 in 5 chance
5) $^3/_4$ or a 3 in 4 chance
6) $^4/_7$ or a 4 in 7 chance
7) $^1/_{10}$ or a 1 in 10 chance
8) $^5/_6$ or a 5 in 6 chance
9) $^5/_8$ or a 5 in 8 chance
10) $^5/_6$ or a 5 in 6 chance

Exercise 14: 6
1) 10%
2) 20%
3) 20%
4) 50%
5) 75%
6) 0.5
7) 0.25
8) 0.4
9) 0.3
10) 0.8

Exercise 14: 7
1) $^1/_5$
2) $^1/_{13}$
3) $^3/_{13}$
4) 20%
5) $^2/_5$
6) $^1/_{10}$
7) $^1/_6$
8) $^2/_5$
9) $^7/_{10}$
10) 0.8

Chapter Fifteen
Lines & Angles
Exercise 15: 1
1) parallel
2) parallel
3) perpendicular
4) vertical
5) diagonal
6) 5
7) 14
8) 7
9) 4
10) 5

Exercise 15: 2
1) a & j
2) No
3) f & i
4) e & h
5) No
6) 4
7) 4
8) No
9) 3
10) Yes

Exercise 15: 3
1) c, g & h
2) b, e, f & i
3) a, d & j
4) acute
5) obtuse
6) reflex
7) acute
8) acute
9) reflex
10) obtuse

© 2016 Stephen Curran   77

Answers

Exercise 15: 4a

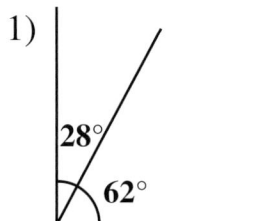

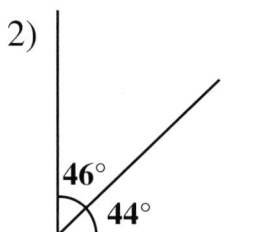

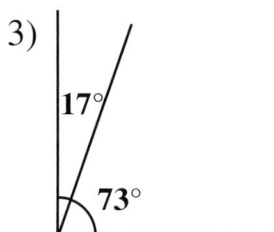

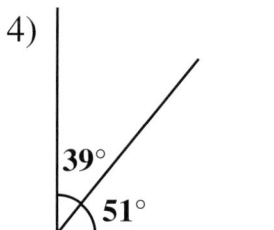

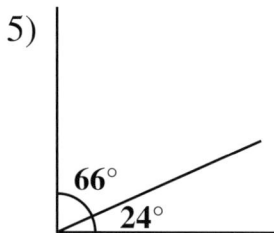

1) 28° 62°

2) 46° 44°

3) 17° 73°

4) 39° 51°

5) 66° 24°

Exercise 15: 4b

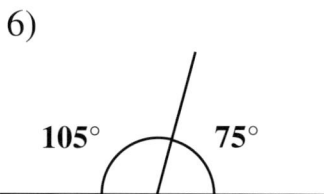

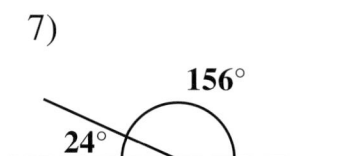

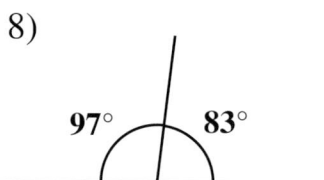

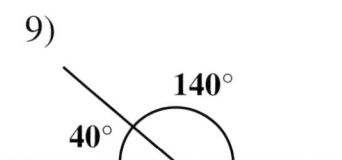

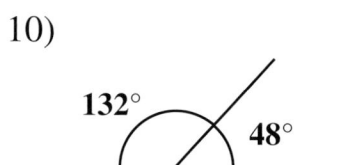

6) 105° 75°

7) 156° 24°

8) 97° 83°

9) 140° 40°

10) 132° 48°

Exercise 15: 5a

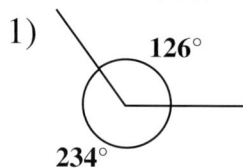

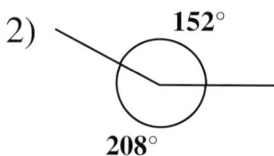

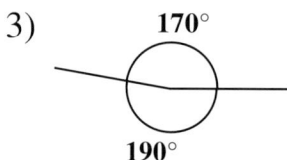

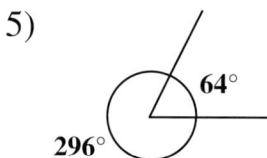

1) 126° 234°

2) 152° 208°

3) 170° 190°

4) 347° 13°

5) 64° 296°

Exercise 15: 5b

6) opposite
7) adjacent
8) adjacent
9) opposite
10) yes

Exercise 15: 6

1) 100° opposite
2) 54° complementary
3) 297° conjugate
4) 78° complementary
5) 63° supplementary
6) 50° conjugate
7) 31° complementary
8) 37° supplementary
9) 59° conjugate
10) 54° supplementary

Exercise 15: 7

1) 45°
2) 60°
3) 75°
4) 150°
5) 105°
6) 117°
7) 24°
8) 58°
9) 40°
10) 83°

Exercise 15: 8

1) 315°
2) North-east
3) South-west
4) 090°
5) 225°
6) 180°
7) 045°
8) South-east
9) East
10) South

PROGRESS CHARTS

Shade in your score for each exercise on the graph. Add up for your total score.

12. PERCENTAGES

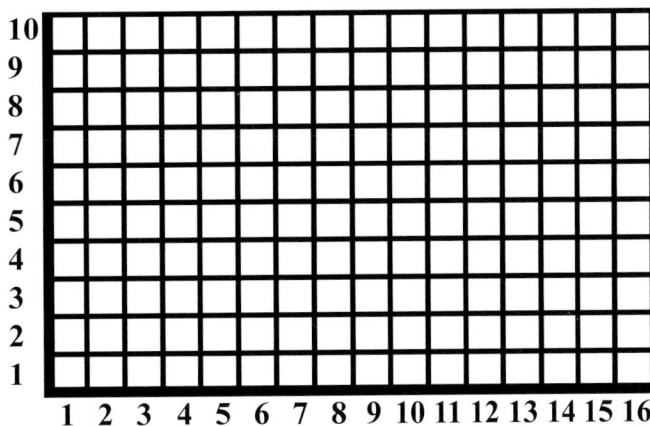

Scores
10 9 8 7 6 5 4 3 2 1

1 2 3 4 5 6 7 8 9 10 11 12 13 14 15 16
Exercises

Total Score

Percentage
%

13. RATIO

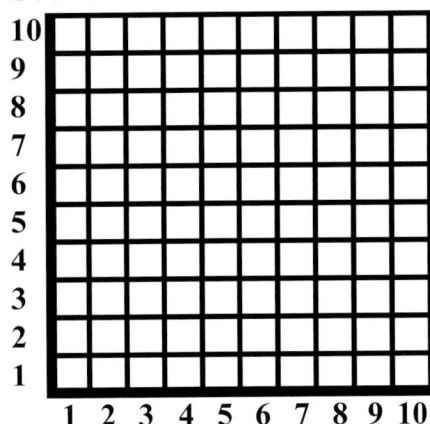

Scores
10 9 8 7 6 5 4 3 2 1

1 2 3 4 5 6 7 8 9 10
Exercises

Total Score

Percentage
%

14. PROBABILITY

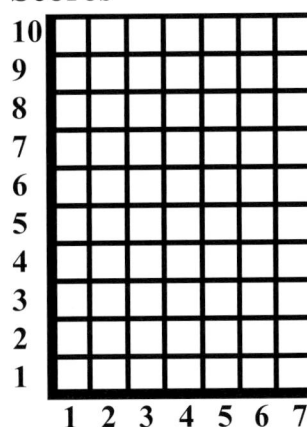

Scores
10 9 8 7 6 5 4 3 2 1

1 2 3 4 5 6 7
Exercises

Total Score

Percentage
%

15. LINES & ANGLES

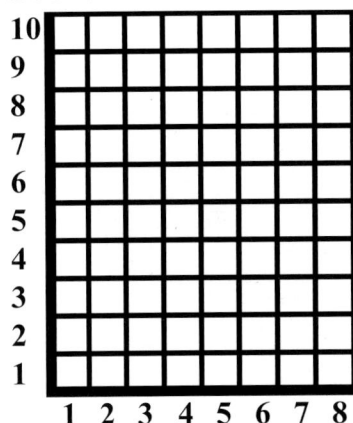

Scores
10 9 8 7 6 5 4 3 2 1

1 2 3 4 5 6 7 8
Exercises

Total Score

Percentage
%

Overall Percentage %

CERTIFICATE OF

ACHIEVEMENT

This certifies

_____

has successfully completed

Key Stage 2 Maths
Year 4/5
WORKBOOK 6

Overall percentage
score achieved

%

Comment _____

_____

Signed _____

(teacher/parent/guardian)

Date _____